Cambridge Elem

Elements in Public Policy
edited by
M. Ramesh
National University of Singapore (NUS)
Michael Howlett
Simon Fraser University, British Colombia
Xun WU
Hong Kong University of Science and Technology
Judith Clifton
University of Cantabria
Eduardo Araral
National University of Singapore (NUS)

PUBLIC POLICY AND UNIVERSITIES

The Interplay of Knowledge and Power

Andrew Gunn
Monash University

Michael Mintrom
Monash University

CAMBRIDGE
UNIVERSITY PRESS

CAMBRIDGE
UNIVERSITY PRESS

University Printing House, Cambridge CB2 8BS, United Kingdom

One Liberty Plaza, 20th Floor, New York, NY 10006, USA

477 Williamstown Road, Port Melbourne, VIC 3207, Australia

314–321, 3rd Floor, Plot 3, Splendor Forum, Jasola District Centre,
New Delhi – 110025, India

103 Penang Road, #05–06/07, Visioncrest Commercial, Singapore 238467

Cambridge University Press is part of the University of Cambridge.

It furthers the University's mission by disseminating knowledge in the pursuit of
education, learning, and research at the highest international levels of excellence.

www.cambridge.org
Information on this title: www.cambridge.org/9781108703666
DOI: 10.1017/9781108645867

First published 2022

A catalogue record for this publication is available from the British Library

ISBN 978-1-108-70366-6 Paperback
ISSN 2398-4058 (online)
ISSN 2514-3565 (print)

Public Policy and Universities

The Interplay of Knowledge and Power

Elements in Public Policy

DOI: 10.1017/9781108645867
First published online: April 2022

Andrew Gunn
Monash University

Michael Mintrom
Monash University

Author for correspondence: Andrew Gunn, Andrew.Gunn@monash.edu

Abstract: Higher education is undergoing unprecedented transformation. In the global knowledge economy, universities are of paramount importance to governments worldwide. This creates a strong rationale for an Element exploring how the interactions between universities and the state are being reconfigured while highlighting the role policy analysis can play in explaining these dynamics. Specifically, this Element draws on four theoretical approaches – New Institutionalism, the Advocacy Coalition Framework, the Narrative Policy Framework, and Policy Diffusion and Transfer – to inform the analysis. Examples are drawn from a range of countries, and areas of potential research informed by policy theory are identified. This Element features a section dedicated to each of the three main missions of the university, followed by an analysis of the institution as a whole. This reveals how universities, while typically seeking greater autonomy, remain subject to a multifaceted form of nation state oversight as they continue to globalise in an uncertain world.

This Element also has a video abstract:
www.cambridge.org/PublicPolicy_Gunn_abstract

Keywords: universities, higher education, policy theory, government, policymaking

ISBNs: 9781108703666 (PB), 9781108645867 (OC)
ISSNs: 2398-4058 (online), 2514-3565 (print)

Contents

1 Public Policy and Universities

1.1 Introduction

Universities are being subject to unprecedented change. Higher education is a large and growing industry worldwide, being reshaped by the processes of globalisation, regionalism, and evolving national contexts. In the global knowledge economy, universities are important institutions, and many governments want to ensure these institutions realise their full potential to maximise the benefits. The complex relationships that surround universities make it difficult to interpret the key drivers of change. That difficulty inhibits the process of clear-eyed planning for the future, both on the part of universities and policymakers.

Many would agree this is a sector that exhibits a high level of 'blooming, buzzing confusion', to appropriate from William James. Universities are being transformed by new dynamics between the state and the market, the public and the private, and the domestic and the global. The interactions between universities and the state are being reconfigured. Accelerated and unprecedented changes in the sector tend to exacerbate the problem of interpretation. This presents a fundamental problem. That is, at the very time when people recognise the important role that universities play in the public sphere, they often find it difficult to deduce what can be done to ensure that universities continue to contribute effectively – and, preferably, at their very best – for stakeholders.

It is beyond the scope of one Element to attempt to explain everything that is happening in and around the contemporary university. For this reason, this Element focusses on the interface where universities and the state meet. This focus produces an Element dedicated to the role of government intervention in higher education, which is why this study sits well within the Cambridge Elements in Public Policy series.

The purpose of this Element is to:

1. illustrate the wide range of policy interventions to which universities are subject;
2. show how the relationship between universities and the state is enduring, evolving, and multifaceted; and
3. demonstrate how policy theory can help explain these dynamics.

This is achieved through an analysis that:

1. features a section dedicated to each of the three 'missions' of the university, followed by a section considering the university as an institution as a whole;

2. illustrates some of the key contemporary policy debates with select examples from countries with contrasting political systems; and
3. develops a conceptual framework informed by theories and insights from recent public policy scholarship and applies this framework to the study of universities.

We show that:

1. a range of factors shape the contemporary university, such as interests beyond both the nation state and the academy that exercise influence, such as foreign states, industry, and other powerful stakeholders;
2. in the face of rhetoric of the deregulation and internationalisation of higher education, there is a continuing role for the nation state in shaping and supporting the university; and
3. our framework can guide future critical analysis of public policy towards universities and future empirical research – we show this through select case examples.

The application of public policy scholarship to the study of the university aids our understanding of the nature of state intervention and the challenges surrounding effective regulation. This Element's distinctive structure and focus allow us to address a significant gap in contemporary public policy scholarship. The Element also seeks to make a contribution to the higher education literature. What is presented here is not intended to provide an exhaustive account of all the interactions between government and universities. The concise yet authoritative format means the examples and theoretical approaches included have been selected from a much larger pool of potential content. Although we expect the Element to be primarily of value to academic scholars, it should also be of use to university leaders and to policymakers and advisers in and around government. This is because the insights generated are of interest to all parties involved in the higher education policy process. For those working in universities, this Element should lead to a greater understanding of the role of the state. For those working in government, it should facilitate a greater appreciation of what is happening within universities.

1.2 Expanded Understandings of What Universities Do

We can conceptualise the university as being comprised of three missions: teaching, research, and the third mission of 'externally facing' functions (Scott, 2006). This accounts for the expanded range of responsibilities the university has assumed over time. This disaggregation into missions, as depicted in Figure 1, has informed the structure of this Element.

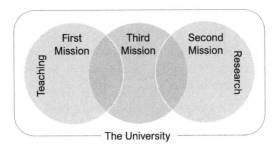

Figure 1 The Three Missions of the University

Looking at the history of the Western university, the first such institutions were focussed on the transmission of knowledge through teaching. These institutions, such as the University of Bologna and the University of Paris, which emerged in the eleventh and twelfth centuries, established important traditions and became known as the original universities. Current debates in the teaching mission are explained in Section 3. The second mission of research did not appear widely inside the university until the creation of the University of Berlin in 1810. This is known as the Humboldtian model of the university, where research and teaching took place in the same institution. The model diffused worldwide and was particularly embraced in the United States (Menand et al., 2017). The research mission is the focus of Section 4. The creation of the land-grant universities in the United States in the second half of the nineteenth century heralded the start of a view that universities should be of relevance to stakeholders around them (Key, 1996). This brings us to Section 5, where we consider the third mission. The third mission is an umbrella term used by contemporary higher education scholars. It refers to the 'externally engaged activities' of the university. It involves a range of activities, from civic engagements to commercialisation of research. Universities have always interacted with the world around them, but the activities that fall under this category are increasingly managed and measured in their own right. Some are quite remote from and not immediately recognisable (at least in a traditional sense) as either teaching or research.

After we have 'zoomed in' to look at each of the three missions in Sections 3–5, we 'zoom out' to consider the university as an institution as a whole in Section 6. Section 7 concludes this Element by reflecting on key debates and by highlighting opportunities for future research on public policy and universities.

1.3 The Plurality of Policy Interventions

A traditional view of higher education policy involves one government ministry benignly providing funds to universities for them to teach students and undertake research. The policymaking behind this was relatively straightforward, with few questions being asked about how funds were spent. This is no longer the case. The complexity of the modern university has met the complexity of the modern state. Within this landscape, a wide range of government activities cross paths with what universities do. This intersection, where universities regularly meet the state, is a deceptively large space that spans ministries, portfolios, policy areas, and political agendas. To illustrate this, we can map out how universities are affected by policy agendas from across the state, well beyond the confines of one ministry. Some of the examples introduced here are elaborated on throughout the Element.

Public servants once would have been occupied with planning student numbers and ensuring there was matching capacity within appropriately resourced public institutions. Although this is still often the case, how this is done has been transformed by new approaches to governance involving innovations such as performance-based funding models (De Boer et al., 2015; Dougherty and Natow, 2015). These changes have also been accompanied by the pressure on policymakers to respond to emerging new agendas, including concerns about freedom of speech on campus; tackling the rise of contract cheating (Draper and Newton, 2017); and designing interventions to address social mobility, equality of opportunity, and affirmative action (Shah et al., 2015; Warikoo and Allen, 2020). Moreover, internationalisation has profoundly changed higher education (de Wit and Altbach, 2021), with ramifications for lawmakers. This includes providing oversight of the growing number of branch campus operations of foreign universities located within their jurisdictions (Clifford and Kinser, 2016).

The funding of student places has also become more complex for the finance or treasury ministry. One trend is the spread of student loan schemes, which are often income-contingent and part-financed from the public purse. They are intended to move more of the costs of a university education from the taxpayer to the individuals who benefit directly from that education. These schemes require more complex accounting to administer than straightforward public spending. Many variables must be managed, such as the repayment rate and threshold, the interest rate, and the level of write off that will never be collected (Chapman et al., 2014; Hillman and Orosz, 2017; Britton et al., 2019). Student loans can also be controversial. For example, in the United States, 40 million people hold student debt totalling $1 trillion, explaining why student loan forgiveness proposals were part of presidential candidate campaign platforms in 2020 (Dynarski, 2021).

Over the last thirty years, what universities do has been of increasing interest to those who influence economic, industrial, and innovation policy. In the context of the knowledge economy, the outputs universities produce speak directly to these policy imperatives. This is done in two ways. First, through their teaching mission, universities produce human capital in the form of graduate labour, which places universities within the high skills and productivity agendas (Pelinescu, 2015). Second, through the research mission, universities produce new knowledge that can be applied to drive innovation (Mintrom, 2009a). This relationship is depicted by the Triple Helix of university–industry–government, which shows the integral role of the university in processes of innovation and entrepreneurship (Etzkowitz and Zhou, 2017). These connections have unleashed a flurry of policy activity upon universities. The interventions are designed to enhance the transfer of knowledge and foster collaborations among universities, government, and firms to generate and commercialise new knowledge for use in industry. Moreover, universities are often allocated a role by policymakers in helping to stimulate the economies of lagging regions within which they are based (Lazzeroni and Piccaluga, 2018; Brennan and Cochrane, 2019).

The business of universities is of interest to foreign ministries, where, in a world of shifting geopolitics, higher education can be used as a tool of 'soft power' by nation states to exercise influence, build new diplomatic and business relationships, and develop cultural exchanges (Altbach and Peterson, 2015; Wojciuk, 2018). This can be seen in the rise of 'science diplomacy' (Flink and Rüffin, 2019) and in schemes such as the UK Government's Newton Fund (Grimes and McNulty, 2016). Higher education policies can also be constructed with a broad foreign policy dimension embedded within them, such as how the Bologna Process was tied to the underlying interests of the European Union (EU) (Moscovitz and Zahavi, 2019).

Policies pursued by the ministry of the interior or home affairs also have a bearing on universities. This is because new academics and visitors coming from outside a given country may require visas to gain entry. In an age of high academic mobility across borders, this is critical for many universities that now view themselves as international organisations. Moreover, through controlling the number of study visas issued, governments determine the number of international students recruited and therefore significantly influence the customer base of universities within their borders. Some international students may expect a work visa upon completion of their studies, pulling discussions about student numbers into the wider skilled migration debate (Hawthorne, 2018; Beech, 2019). The importance of the border was highlighted during the COVID-19 pandemic in countries such as Australia, where international students were restricted from entering, thus exposing the high financial dependence of many universities on this income (Doidge and Doyle, 2020).

Public managers within ministries of business regulation and trade – such as the Antitrust Division of the US Department of Justice – will also find themselves concerned with higher education. This is because market competition and consumer protection have to be upheld while collusion and the mis-selling of degree programmes and student finance need to be policed. In many countries, the number of profit-making higher education businesses offering degrees has been increasing, creating regulatory challenges for policymakers (Salop and White, 1991; Mause, 2010; Tierney, 2012).

We can see there are a plethora of policy debates affecting universities prompted by different components of the 'machinery of government'. This matters because the concept of 'departmentalism' tells us each government department can have a particular 'mindset' or an accumulated 'wisdom' that shapes how policy is made (Kavanagh and Richards, 2001; d'Ombrain, 2007). Moreover, each policy issue has its own imperatives and is therefore potentially subject to influence by issue-related interest groups. This can explain why the policy interventions universities experience can be the product of several competing, possibly contradictory, priorities. This lack of coherence means university leaders often find themselves responding to conflicting demands from government. The presence of multiple interventions influencing universities in a given territory, rather than a single higher education policy, needs to be acknowledged when undertaking policy analysis in this area.

1.4 Academic Literatures

The relationship between universities and the state is continuously changing, as is the broader context in which both universities and governments operate. In seeking to explore this, we recognise that there are many useful scholarly contributions in the extant literature. Although the focus of this Element is centred on policy analysis, there are two adjacent literatures that help explain why and how interactions between universities and the state are being reconfigured.

The first is the growing importance of knowledge creation and diffusion as the core driver of economic growth. In economics, the arrival of endogenous growth theories – which maintain that improvements in productivity can be attributed to investments in human capital and research and development (Acs and Sanders, 2021) – placed universities as a crucial determinant in the growth process. This is because intellectual capital is now seen as being of rising importance in delivering economic growth when compared to traditional factors such as natural resources, physical capital, and low-skilled labour. The idea of the knowledge economy is more than economic theory; it is a story, a narrative that, despite being somewhat illusive, has been extensively told and widely accepted (Brinkley, 2006; Mintrom, 2009a).

This idea of a global race to a knowledge economy has diffused around the world, often advocated by influential international organisations – such as the Organisation for Economic Co-operation and Development (OECD), the World Bank, the World Trade Organisation – who have set a common global direction for government policies (Maskus, 2004; Robertson, 2009). The OECD has been an effective disseminator of the narrative, which has been used to frame policy change around the world (Godin 2004, 2006). The OECD defines the 'knowledge-based economy' as 'an expression coined to describe trends in advanced economies towards greater dependence on knowledge, information and high skill levels, and the increasing need for ready access to all of these by the business and public sectors' (OECD, 2005). The narrative is particularly compelling as it issues a call for action to both nation states and individuals. It encourages policymakers to enhance their national economic competitiveness by expanding university participation, as there is the belief that the future workforce needs to be more highly skilled and be able to compete in a global labour market (Craig and Gunn, 2010). The narrative also suggests states need to invest in research and its application to drive technological change and innovation. In some respects, universities have been the beneficiaries of this narrative. Although academics may show disdain towards universities being a facet of the knowledge economy, rather than being for the pursuit of knowledge for its own sake, the narrative has leveraged a considerable amount of money into universities. It is worth thinking how it might unravel if governments and individuals started to question the value of university education or the benefits of publicly funded research.

The literature on Academic Capitalism shows moving universities closer to the market has been consequential (Slaughter and Leslie, 1997; Slaughter and Rhoades, 2004). The political economy context has been transformed, as Jessop (2018) explains, where universities 'act less like centers of disinterested education and research and more like economic enterprises that aim to maximize their revenues and/or advance the economic competitiveness of the spaces in which they operate'. This development has become more global because of intensifying competition among relevant institutions and the wider economic and political spaces in which they are embedded, and the tendency for actors to follow the latest trends.

The second adjacent literature, which helps explain why and how interactions between universities and the state are being reconfigured, can be placed under the Regulatory Governance heading. We see a trend towards governments around the world intensifying the regulation and monitoring of universities.

This is taking place at a time when the authority of the state, its mode of collective decision-making, its use of bureaucratic command and control steering approaches, and its role in public higher education have been increasingly questioned by interest groups, candidates for political office, and citizens alike. Despite its different forms and foci, public sector reform has been a common experience across the globe (Pollitt and Bouckaert, 2004). In this process, higher education has been subject to the same reform agenda as other sectors, a common theme being the application of New Public Management (NPM) ideas through public policy to universities (Capano, 2011; Dobbins et al., 2011). This has resulted in a shift from a 'state-control' to a 'state-supervising' model of university steering, which is accompanied by the deployment of performance assessment instruments (see Lumino et al., 2017 and Duque, 2021 as examples). Here, the role of the state has become 'evaluative' rather than 'directive' (Neave, 2012). This has resulted in new and less hierarchical relationships between government and universities, from which more market-oriented and complex organisational models have emerged (Teixeira et al., 2014).

In this context, many governments, to varying degrees, are prepared to continue financing universities, but they are not prepared to write a blank cheque and pay scant attention to results. Policymakers are increasingly being instructed to produce innovative measures of productivity and quality for universities. The resource provider role places the state in a powerful position. It shifts the relationship with universities from 'you'll do what we *say* you'll do' to 'you'll do what we *pay* you to do'.

The extent to which the state can influence universities often rests on the robustness of the 'mediating forces' of institutional autonomy and academic freedom. The strength of this 'buffer zone', in principle and in practice, varies between countries and is typically a product of political systems and higher education histories. The 'buffer zone' means higher education policy often differs from other policy areas – such as compulsory education or policing – where more direct forms of intervention are deployed and regarded as acceptable. Where policymakers do not wish to – or do not have the means to – implement government objectives directly on universities, the indirect steering instruments associated with NPM are very useful. Here, policy involves setting goals and parameters and letting incentives drive university responses.

1.5 The Relevance of the Nation and National Politics

Although overarching trends are evident, the relationship between universities and government varies considerably. Some of these differences can be attributed to alternative economic systems, such as if we compare the United States with the People's Republic of China (PRC) on the role of central planning in shaping higher education or the freedom of universities to lobby government. Alternatively, universities may be treated differently after changes in domestic politics, such as a change in governing party or leader. A pertinent example here is the treatment of universities in Hungary during the premiership of Viktor Orbán (Enyedi, 2018). Changes to Hungarian law between 2011 and 2014 saw the government exerting greater central control over the appointments of rectors and chancellors. Following this, the government attacked the Central European University (CEU) by prohibiting it from maintaining its dual Hungarian and American legal identity. This ultimately resulted in the CEU relocating to Austria. Corbett and Gordon (2019) note this can be explained by the incompatibility between the CEU – which was founded in 1991 to promote the democratic values of an open society in former communist countries – and the authoritarian turn in Hungarian politics described by Orbán as his 'illiberal democracy'. Corbett and Gordon also find this is not an isolated case. The rise of populist governments has seen ten countries in Central and Eastern Europe – all EU members – using legal instruments to restrict university autonomy, with adverse effects for academic freedom. Orbán's unorthodox policy interventions would continue when, after expelling a US private university, the government invited a state-controlled Chinese university to open a campus. An attractive offer was made to Fudan University in 2021, including donating state-owned land to develop a big-budget campus in Budapest. The offer was made in spite of criticism it would undermine existing Hungarian universities and was a vehicle for Beijing to increase its influence on Hungary and Europe (Komuves, 2021).

This illustrates how many universities operate internationally. It is also a reminder that how universities are treated by the state is not merely about technocratic policy instruments. Rather, it is also determined by more fundamental political attributes such as the *quality* of democracy and how the state uses the rule of law (Diamond and Morlino 2004; O'Donnell, 2004). Politics, and their bearing on policy, matter. The role of national politics underscores the importance of theoretically informed policy research being undertaken concerning universities at the level of the nation state. This remains an imperative in the context of globalisation.

1.6 Conclusion

As universities and their operating contexts have become more complex, policy interventions have also become more multifaceted. Moreover, whether in the public or private sector, irrespective of funding sources or the presence of the profit motive, universities require appropriate regulatory oversight. For governments, this presents a set of new challenges to develop policy applicable to this rapidly changing sector. Given these complexities, those studying contemporary universities can sharpen their assessments through deployment of concepts and tools that are the stock in trade of policy analysts. To demonstrate this, Section 2 introduces a selection of theoretical approaches.

2 A Theoretical Framework

2.1 Introduction

Throughout this Element, we apply insights emanating from theories of the policy process. The development of policy theory encompasses a large intellectual discussion featuring a growing range of approaches (Weible and Sabatier, 2018). The format of this Element means only some aspects of this literature can be included. Specifically, New Institutionalism, the Advocacy Coalition Framework, the Narrative Policy Framework, and Policy Diffusion and Transfer have been selected for our theoretical framework (see Figure 2). Taken together, these four theories shed light upon the institutions and interest groups involved as well as the power of ideas and how they spread around the world. These four approaches have been adopted as they are most applicable to the content featured in Sections 3–6. This section introduces each approach in turn with examples of how they have been applied to the study of higher education more widely. It should be noted that other theories of the policy process are suitable for deployment in understanding many different pieces of higher education research, well beyond what is presented here.

2.2 New Institutionalism

In 1983, March and Olsen began a renaissance in the study of institutions with their seminal article, *New Institutionalism: Organizational Factors in*

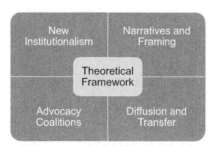

Figure 2 A theoretical framework

Political Life. Since then, a large literature on the New Institutionalism has developed, producing numerous offshoots. Of particular relevance to this Element is Historical Institutionalism as it accounts for continuity and changes over time.

Within the New Institutionalism, institutions are understood as the 'rules of the game', which serve to provide stability and certainty to those operating within them. Rules are 'routines, procedures, conventions, roles, strategies, organisational forms and technologies around which political activity is constructed' (March and Olsen, 1989, p. 22). Alongside formal rules exist informal norms of behaviour that serve to steer the behaviours of actors within the institutional structures. There is interplay between structure and agency and two logics at work that govern the behaviour of actors and organisations: the logic of appropriateness that is juxtaposed with the logic of expected consequences (Goldmann, 2005). The logic of appropriateness suggests that 'behaviours (beliefs as well as actions) are intentional but not wilful. They involve fulfilling the obligations of a role in a situation, and so of trying to determine the imperatives of holding a position' (March and Olsen, 1989, p. 160). The logic of appropriateness sees the actions of individuals as being driven by rules of appropriate or exemplary behaviour as conditioned by institutions. The rules of the game are adhered to because they are seen as natural, rightful, expected, and legitimate. Actors seek to meet the obligations that come from membership of a group, and they adhere to the ethos, practices, and expectations of that institution. The logic of appropriateness is set against the logic of expected consequences that accounts for the self-interested actions of rational actors who have fixed preferences and identities. The logic of expected consequences sees the behaviour of individuals as determined by the calculation of expected returns from alternative choices.

Using this framework, Olsen (2007) construes the university as an institution, while Meyer et al. (2008) construe higher education as an institution. Both conceptions are compatible because one set of institutions can often be nested within another (Mintrom, 2009a). A particularly useful concept is that of path dependency. This is where, once established, a particular path becomes a self-reinforcing process (Pierson, 2004; Kay, 2005). The concept is relevant to this study as Bhattacharya (2012) explains:

> The university is a path-dependent institution, not least because today's faculty were trained yesterday, in a sequence that goes back eight centuries. The institution's function and structure have been shaped by a particular set of historical conditions. Some of these constructs from earlier times remain today, engendering contemporary conflicts that we cannot grasp without viewing them in a diachronic frame (Bhattacharya, 2012, p. 208).

Path dependency is useful in explaining how the university as an institution endures. For example, in a study of German universities, Krücken (2003) finds learning new things and change to be a 'more cumbersome process than might be expected', which can be explained by the path-dependent character of institutional structures, practices, and identities. This explains how the rapid change at the level of higher education discourse does not always translate into practice within universities. However, we should not assume universities stay the same. Institutions may incrementally change over time, even during periods of stability in the world around them. Moreover, events at a critical juncture, where the established equilibrium is broken, can result in more significant or sudden change. In this Element, we show how public policy change can drive change in universities through tweaking the rules of the game, thus introducing new logics and disrupting established routines.

Another relevant branch of institutionalism is DiMaggio and Powell's (1983) work on Institutional Isomorphism, where coercive, mimetic, and normative forces result in organisations becoming increasingly similar over time. Writing in the early 1980s, the authors saw how the drivers of rationalisation and bureaucratisation had moved from the competitive marketplace to the state and the professions. They observed 'that once a set of organisations emerges as a field, a paradox arises: rational actors make their organizations increasingly similar as they try to change them'. This is of particular relevance to today's university, and institutional isomorphism has been widely observed in research (see Joo et al., 2012; Croucher and Woelert, 2016; Dobbins and Knill, 2017; Seyfried et al., 2019). In Section 6 we focus on how in the context of globalisation many universities seek to emulate one global model.

There is also Network Institutionalism, which considers institutions as being in a network involving a 'stable or recurrent pattern of behavioral interaction or exchange between individuals or organizations' (Ansell, 2008, p. 75). Ansell (2008) argues 'a network can be distinguished both by the content of relationships (positive recurrent relations, built on mutual obligations, affection, trust, and reciprocity, etc.) and by its global structure (interconnected dyads, many-to-many relationships)' (Ansell, 2008, p. 78). This draws our attention to how universities formally collaborate, which we explore in Section 6.

2.3 Advocacy Coalitions

The Advocacy Coalition Framework was developed by Paul Sabatier (1988) who defined advocacy coalitions as comprising people 'who share a particular belief system – for example, a set of basic values, causal assumptions, and problem perceptions – and who show a nontrivial degree of coordinated activity over time'. Sabatier rejected the traditional view in political science that legislators and interest group leaders are politically active in seeking to influence public policy, while agency officials, researchers, and journalists were more passive or indifferent to policy change. He argued all these strategic actions of individuals, regardless of organisational affiliation, can contribute to common policy objectives and therefore should be considered in a study of policymaking processes.

Over the past thirty years, the Advocacy Coalition Framework has been refined by Sabatier and colleagues (Sabatier and Jenkins-Smith, 1993; Sabatier, 1998). It has been applied by hundreds of scholars (Jenkins-Smith et al., 2018; Weible et al., 2020). The framework rests on the assumptions that individuals are boundedly rational (instrumental, but cognitively limited) with complex normative and empirical 'belief systems' and that they pursue policy change to realise specific beliefs. Furthermore, these actors will increase their chances of success by embedding themselves in specific 'policy subsystems' and coordinating with others who share similar beliefs (Luxon, 2019, p. 106). A 'policy subsystem' is the unit of analysis that is defined by a policy topic, a geographical scope, and the actors who are actively concerned with influencing the policy issue. Policy change can be viewed as the translation of the belief systems of the winning coalition(s) in a subsystem into policy action.

The Advocacy Coalition Framework encourages us to look very widely at the actors and interests surrounding policymaking. This is particularly useful when looking for the voices influencing higher education policy, as many of these originate from outside either universities or the state. For example, Harnisch (2016) investigates how business-led advocacy coalitions were developed, used, and maintained to advance higher education as a state budgetary priority in Michigan and Virginia in the United States. In a study of Brazilian higher education, Balbachevsky (2015) applied the framework to map the alliances between the large number of internal and external stakeholders, each holding diverging values and expectations. This revealed the interplay between the main advocacy coalitions and the resulting controversies and convergences in the debate over future policy.

2.4 The Narrative Policy Framework

The Narrative Policy Framework is a relatively new theory that has been developed through a proliferation of research applications since its inception (Jones and McBeth, 2010). It seeks to account for the power and influence of narrative in the policy process and is therefore related to the more established theory of framing. This lens brings the perspectives of social construction to an analysis of policy. In Section 1 we introduced the knowledge economy as a contemporary policy narrative.

The Narrative Policy Framework is comprised of form and content. Form has four elements: first, the context in which a policy problem resides; second, the characters that are socially constructed as victims, villains, or heroes; third, the plot that maps the relationships between the characters; and fourth, the moral of the story, which is the takeaway of a policy narrative and often refers to the ethical aspects of the policy solution proposed within the plot (Stone, 2012). The framework has five underlying assumptions. First, the social constructions people use to interpret and define politics and policy matter. This is where an important part of reality is not so much what is, but rather what people believe something means. Second, bounded rationality, where the ability of people to determine what something means is limited. Because of this, people will hold, seek out, or invent ways of interpreting something based on their beliefs or ideologies. Third, policy narratives have generalisable components, meaning they are 'things' that exist in the world discrete from other objects and therefore can be counted. Fourth, narratives operate at three interacting levels: individual, group, and cultural/institutional. Fifth, storytelling is given primacy over reasoning. The framework assumes people are not just creatures of reason, rather emotion precedes reasoning. This enables narratives to influence decision-making (Jones, 2018, p. 727; Shanahan, Jones et al., 2018, p. 332).

We can see the overlap here to the theory of framing that 'refers to the process by which people develop a particular conceptualization of an issue or reorient their thinking about an issue' (Chong and Druckman, 2007, p. 104). Frames can be seen as 'objects people possess in their heads and develop for explicitly strategic purposes' while framing is 'the interactive, intersubjective processes through which frames are constructed' (van Hulst and Yanow, 2016, p. 93). König (2019) notes that how policies are communicated, or framed, has become an important aspect in explaining their occurrence and success. Framing is therefore a powerful instrument in the hands of policy actors, who need to establish a particular interpretation of a policy in public discourse and help to 'sell' change to the public. Useful linkages can be drawn between the Narrative Policy Framework and the Advocacy Coalition Framework (Crow and Lawlor, 2016). An important question also arises concerning how policy narratives move between countries and carry policy change with them, as explained by policy diffusion and transfer.

2.5 Policy Diffusion and Transfer

The process by which policies move between different nations and organisations has a long history and has gone under many different labels (Walker, 1969;

Rose, 1993; Stone, 2019). The ideas in Everett M. Rogers' (1962) seminal book *Diffusion of Innovations* were influential in thinking about how new ideas become more widely adopted and went on to be incorporated into the study of policy diffusion (Makse and Volden, 2011). Policy diffusion research flourished (Graham, 2013), showing diffusion taking place across different jurisdictions of one nation (Abel, 2019), and increasingly between different countries (Ceccoli and Crosston, 2019; True and Mintrom, 2001).

Simmons et al. (2006) define international policy diffusion as a process that 'occurs when government policy decisions in a given country are systematically conditioned by prior policy choices made in other countries (sometimes mediated by the behaviour of international organizations or private actors and organizations)' (Simmons et al., 2006, p. 787). These ideas are of relevance to this Element because we are interested in how perceived policy problems and proposed policy solutions have spread around the world.

Related to policy diffusion is the concept of policy transfer, which is also known as policy borrowing. Marsh and Sharman (2009) explain 'the literatures on policy transfer and policy diffusion are complementary', although there are some methodological differences between the two. Both literatures identify four mechanisms: first, learning, where governments make a 'rational' decision to emulate foreign practice as these measures produce more efficient and effective policy outcomes. Second, competition, where governments need to ensure their economies remain competitive in a global marketplace by keeping pace with rivals' domestic policies. Third, coercion, which may come from powerful states who can exert pressure from donors who attach conditions to their support. Fourth, mimicry where policymakers emulate foreign models that symbolically seem to be more advanced, rather than a technical or rational concern with functional efficiency (Marsh and Sharman, 2009, p. 271–272).

International organisations often play a large role in policy diffusion, through their support of cross-jurisdictional learning, rather than through coercion (Sellar and Lingard, 2013; Carroll, 2014; Nay, 2014). In education policy, the OECD is particularly influential. For example, in a study of vocational education policy in Australia, Le Grand and Vas (2014) explained the substantial, yet unacknowledged, influence of the OECD on policy transfer process through framing policy analysis. Research is not confined to studies of international organisations and can also identify factors that impede policy diffusion. For example, Ballerini (2017) identified 'unique manifestations of global trends' in Argentina, owing to its particular political and academic traditions that inhibited local conformity to global trends.

2.6 Conclusion

The theories outlined in this section guide our analysis in Sections 3–5 as we review some current developments in the teaching, research, and third missions of the university. We also refer to the framework in Section 6 when we consider the university as a whole. In Section 7 we reflect on the theoretical framework as part of the conclusion to the Element. The key features of the four theories – the actors, institutions, ideas, assumptions, and relationships between concepts – guided our selection of content in the subsequent sections. What follows is not an exhaustive application of these theories but a synthesis illustrating the power of policy and a way of organising an analysis of the university that illuminates the political influences acting upon it.

3 The Teaching Mission of the University

3.1 Introduction

The modern university as an institution has its origins in ancient Europe. The Middle Ages saw the foundation of two archetypal universities: the University of Bologna – the oldest continually operating university in the world today – that began in 1088 and the University of Paris that attained formal recognition in the early thirteenth century. Both of these universities were teaching institutions, and they remained the most influential and dominant models of the university for several hundred years. This origin of universities as teaching institutions has given rise to the convention of viewing teaching as the first mission of the university.

But while teaching may be considered the first mission of the university, it does not follow that it is now regarded as the most important when compared to the other two missions – research and engagement. Although it is the biggest business for most universities, the teaching mission is frequently almost 'taken-for-granted' as a merely routine activity. Within the academic profession, teaching is often the 'poor relation' compared to research and confers less esteem upon those who undertake it than the output of research activities (Gunn, 2022).

After introducing the key components of the teaching mission and how they have changed, this section proceeds to look at three contemporary issues. Of particular interest to a study of the interplay of knowledge and power between universities and government are policy issues where the two sides have conflicting ideas on the same problem. To explore these tensions, we juxtapose policy debates around safeguarding academic integrity, a growing problem where governments showed hesitancy and complacency (Section 3.3), with policy debates around protecting freedom of speech, a disputed issue where governments have been keen to intervene (Section 3.4). This is followed by looking at growing national security concerns and how they affect the teaching mission (Section 3.5). We then consider current trends in how the teaching mission is funded and evaluated (Section 3.6). These issues have been selected as they identify the political aspects of the contemporary teaching mission, how the mission is drawn into wider societal debates, and the difficulties that arise when developing policy solutions.

3.2 Key Elements of the Teaching Mission

The teaching mission is broader than the practice of teaching. This rests on the distinction between *teaching in a university* and the *teaching mission of the university*. The former is largely concerned with pedagogy, while the latter is a broader entity, incorporating the inputs, processes, outputs, and outcomes stages of the whole student life cycle. The teaching mission includes student recruitment, applicant information, entry requirements, and widening participation; the student experience and teaching quality within a course, as well as the resources available to learners both online and on campus; outputs such as student retention, credentialing, and grading; and outcomes including graduate destinations and personal development (Gunn, 2018a, p. 135).

The knowledge economy narrative has shaped the teaching mission of universities in recent decades. For example, it has been used to justify the expansion in participation. The 'massification' of higher education has resulted in many countries being 'high participation systems' (Cantwell et al., 2018) – where the percentage of young people entering higher education increased over time and can be a majority of the population. Today, university teaching is a big business as, in addition to this domestic market, the student population on many campuses is augmented by a large number of international students. The knowledge economy imperative has also guided how policymakers think about various aspects of the teaching mission. For example, the employability agenda, which emphasises the need for 'job-ready graduates', has influenced the behaviour of both students and universities.

The teaching mission is also being subject to new forms of disruption. How teaching is delivered is undergoing transformation. As universities seek to expand and reach new student markets, they have opened branch campuses in other territories and offered courses online. This breaks the traditional geography-bound nature of the university. Drivers of this change vary between territories, but several common factors are evident. Changes in the domestic environment have seen many universities dealing with reduced funding from public sources. This has caused them to look elsewhere to bolster student numbers and find new revenue streams. In places such as the United States, these challenges have been accompanied by domestic demographic decline, which has reduced their customer base and more fierce global competition for international students. An example that encapsulates many features of this changing context is the rise of 'mega-universities' in the United States. Mega-universities can be differentiated from other providers by their large enrolments, greater than 80,000. Southern New Hampshire and Western Governors University are examples, where established universities have expanded and diversified their businesses. The business model comes from the fact that the United States is a mature high participation system with low levels of student retention, which has compounded over time to create a large pool of people who never graduated but have some sort of credit – and at some point may wish to resume their studies. In any one locality this might be quite a small number of people, but taken across the United States as a whole it amounts to a large potential market. Although mega universities have their existing physical campuses, they are offering these returning students degrees online meaning they can enrol from anywhere. Digital delivery allows for asynchronous learning that allows greater learner flexibility, and is generally cheaper to deliver, making the courses more affordable. Mega universities have also embraced 'competency-based education', in which students earn credits from life experiences and from demonstrating prior learning in a subject (Gardner, 2019). The factors driving the rise of mega universities illustrate many of the recent trends policymakers and established universities have to contend with.

3.3 Academic Integrity

Academic integrity is the commitment to and demonstration of honest and moral behaviour. Bretag (2016) views academic integrity as a 'multifaceted and multi-stakeholder issue, premised on actions underpinned by values and something which goes well beyond sensationalized scandals of student cheating, plagiarism, and essay mills' (p. 4). Academic integrity has grown in visibility in recent years amid reports that 'contract cheating' has risen (Clarke and Lancaster, 2006) – facilitated by technological change that enables students to purchase assignments online, typically from 'essay mills'. Contract cheating does not just undermine the credentialing function of the university but the entire learning experience. Walker and Townley (2012) point out this new form of cheating 'is a concern to educators because it is very difficult to detect, because it is arguably more fraudulent than some other forms of plagiarism, and because it appears to be connected to a range of systemic problems within modern higher education'. Since publication of Walker and Townley's article, the problem has continued to grow and has been extensively explored within news reports and academic literature (Draper et al., 2017; Medway et al., 2018). Walker and Townley's (2012) study contained recommendations for how universities and educators should respond to contract cheating; however, changes in institutional and professional practices only have limited effect.

Writing in the United States, Drinan (2016) explains why academic integrity has a low political profile, but is an important issue to be addressed. Drinan suggests that new political alliances are 'required to strengthen institutionalisation of academic integrity on campuses' (p. 1075). In recent years we can see as contract cheating grew as a problem in the United States, it received more media attention (see Stockman and Mureithi, 2019, for example). This raised the profile of the issue and initiated action. At least seventeen states across the United States now have some form of law to address contract cheating. This identifies how policy solutions can diffuse across different states in the absence of federal action.

New Zealand was an early mover to legislate in 2011 when it made it illegal to either advertise or provide cheating services (Draper and Newton, 2017). As an example of international policy transfer, this legislation was used as a model when Ireland developed a law that came into effect in 2020 (D'Arcy, 2020). In Australia, media outrage ensued in 2014–15 from the *MyMaster* scandal, when it was found that 1,000 students from sixteen Australian universities had used the Sydney-based ghostwriting service (Kennedy, 2015). Here, the high level of media attention helped articulate the case for government intervention. However, it took several years for this to be implemented with an amendment to an act taking effect in 2020. This law change meant those caught selling cheating services to an Australian student can to face up to two years imprisonment or fines of up to AU$100,000.

In the United Kingdom, lawmakers have been hesitant to address the issue of contract cheating and initially pursued non-legislative solutions to address this problem. However, this approach proved to be insufficient. This provides an interesting example of where the higher education community – which typically desires greater autonomy from the state – has invited governments to intervene. In 2018, forty-five university leaders wrote to the education minister requesting action, and in 2019 a parliament petition was used to draw attention to the issue. Both resulted in no immediate action meaning essay mills were still legal in the United Kingdom during the COVID-19 pandemic, when, with isolated students working remotely, they boomed. This reaffirmed that government intervention was overdue. In early 2021, a former universities minister became a critical actor by introducing the Essay Mills (Prohibition) Bill in the House of

Commons. This was a move from outside the government, as at this time government was preoccupied with addressing free speech on campus.

3.4 Culture Wars

An issue that has risen to public prominence in recent years is that of free speech on campus. Staley (2019) points out:

> Throughout history, debates surrounding freedom of speech on campus commonly revolve around one of three essential questions: first, how do the role and situation of a university affect its responsibility toward speech and expression? Secondly, what kind of responsibility do universities have in providing a diverse curriculum? In other words, is there ever an instance in which a university is justified in censoring a certain person's or group's ideas and beliefs? Lastly, do topics or situations exist that are so controversial that unchecked expression could instigate harm, thereby forcing universities to intervene? (p. 47).

We can see this is not one issue but a sprawling series of debates that can be both complex and controversial. This has wide ramifications as it provides an enormous range of opportunities for individuals or groups to take one aspect and frame it from a particular perspective. Its breadth and intricacy also open the potential for the three different dimensions being conflated or confused. For example, academic freedom and freedom of speech may be used interchangeably when they are not the same thing, while critiques may cite the 'left wing' or 'liberal' tendencies of the academic profession when claiming universities do not provide a diverse curriculum.

Considerable criticism has been levelled at universities for not protecting free speech. This is often triggered by instances of what are referred to as 'cancel culture' or 'no platforming' – where a talk on campus may be cancelled and the speaker not given a platform in the face of opposition or criticism of their appearance. The criticism has escalated into a 'culture war', and various aspects of this debate have materialised in several countries as the state of 'moral panic' has spread (Corbett, 2021).

It is beyond the scope of this section to outline each nuance of what are referred to as the culture wars. But what is of relevance to this Element is how it is possible for groups outside the university to manufacture a purported 'crisis' within it, and then use this as the framing to lobby for government legislation. The crisis can be seen as manufactured because even if we accept there are legitimate grievances it is a disproportionate response. Moreover, these issues have not been ignored by universities as they are an implicit part of their everyday operations. For example, the University of Chicago *Report of the*

Committee on Freedom of Expression – which has subsequently been adopted by numerous universities – highlights the serious attention the issue has received in the United States.

The United States provides a prime example when the conservative youth advocacy group *Turning Point USA* made protecting free speech on college campuses its number one issue. Its leader, Charlie Kirk, actively promoted the idea that US universities are infected with liberal bias that has 'suffocated the free exchange of ideas and helped indoctrinate an entire generation to hate America'. *Turning Point USA* also launched a 'Professor Watchlist' to 'expose and document college professors who discriminate against conservative students and advance leftist propaganda in the classroom'. Kirk's campaign has been credited with instigating President Trump's March 2019 executive order to protect free speech on college campuses (Scatamburlo-D'Annibale, 2019).

Stories of free speech being 'shut down' in Australia resulted in the Minister for Education commissioning an independent review into freedom of speech in higher education in 2018 (Gelber, 2020). The French review, undertaken by a former Chief Justice of the High Court of Australia, found no evidence of a 'free speech crisis' on Australian campuses. In the report, French (2019) did, however, find some ambiguity around the issue and proposed a 'model code' to ensure both 'freedom of lawful speech' and 'academic freedom', which the report clearly differentiates. The government then moved to change terminology in existing legislation of 'free intellectual inquiry' to 'freedom of speech and academic freedom' and enshrine a definition of 'academic freedom' in an act of parliament. Although adoption of the code was voluntary, it was implemented by all universities. Following this, further ministerial action was deemed necessary, and in 2020 the minister commissioned another review into the precise nature of the implementation of the model code within universities. This review rated the extent to which each university aligned its statutory frameworks with the principles of the code.

A parallel set of events took place in the United Kingdom. In response to reports of speakers being de-platformed on campus (Schraer and Butcher, 2018), sector leaders agreed in 2018 to create new guidance that was published by the *Equality and Human Rights Commission* (Equality and Human Rights Commission, 2019). However, the issue was not seen as resolved. In 2019, Theos, the ecumenical think tank, commissioned YouGov to conduct polling on public views of universities, which found 52 per cent thought free speech was under threat in universities. Later in 2019, the Conservative Party election manifesto contained a commitment to 'strengthen academic freedom and free speech in universities' (Conservative Party, 2019, p. 37). In 2020 Policy Exchange, the right-leaning British think tank published a report explaining how universities face growing threats to academic freedom (Adekoya et al., 2020). This resulted in the government publishing a White Paper in 2021 dedicated to how the government would seek to strengthen freedom of speech and academic freedom in higher education. The actions include powers to fine universities and appoint a 'free speech champion' and 'to stamp out unlawful silencing on campuses'. Bekhradnia (2021) argues the White Paper is contributing to culture wars 'imported from Trump and his allies on the libertarian right in the USA', and that, within it, 'sweeping assertions are made primarily on the basis of a small number of anecdotes, press reports and unspecified concerns'.

France provides an example of a larger culture war in society spilling over into higher education. This concerns a culture war that politicians want to be seen actively addressing for electoral reasons. For example, President Emmanuel Macron's government stepped up its political and rhetorical offensive against 'Islamo-gauchisme' to prevent the right capitalising on the issue (Macron, 2020). Islamo-gauchisme is a term frequently used in the French right-wing press that refers to Islamist extremists being enabled by the democratic liberalism of left-leaning intellectuals. Universities were dragged into this political battleground throughout 2020 as French political elites attacked intellectual 'ideological abuses' and 'complicities with terrorism'. French lawmakers legislated for student movements – such as taking part in gatherings – to potentially be criminalised and proposed, but later dropped, provisions in legislation for stating that academic freedom should be exercised with 'respect of the values of the Republic'. (Diallo, 2020). In 2021, the higher education minister announced an investigation into Islamo-gauchisme in French universities. Those advocating this decision pointed to media reports of de-platforming (France 24, 2019). However, hundreds of academics called for the minister to resign for 'defaming a profession'. The organisation representing the presidents of French universities responded that Islamo-gauchisme is not a proper concept but a pseudo-notion, while the organisations instructed to undertake the inquiry called it the 'political exploitation' of a 'political slogan' that does 'not correspond to any scientific reality' (CNRS, 2021).

In the French example, the content of the curriculum has been criticised, in particular some social science subjects have been portrayed as 'corrupting' the secular society of the Republic. This is illustrated by an opinion piece, published in *Le Monde* (2020), by 100 scholars showing their public support of the minister who argued freedom of speech has been drastically restricted and censored by pressure groups while intellectual conformism, fear, and political correctness are a real threat to universities. The op-ed attributed this to the importation of 'anti-Western', 'racialist', and 'decolonial' ideologies from North American campuses that contribute to undermine the idea of the

Republic. These arguments can be used to delegitimise the teaching of some subjects such as post-colonialism, gender, and race studies (Onishi and Meheut, 2021).

This section shows the applicability of the Narratives Policy Framework introduced in Section 2.4. We can see the context of the 'problem' is the modern university. Liberal academics are construed as the 'villains', conservative students and the public as the 'victims', and the advocacy coalitions raising the issue as the 'heroes'. The 'plot' is the violation of free speech and academic freedom on campus and the 'solution' is government intervention. It is an example of storytelling having primacy over reasoning as so much is socially constructed and based on beliefs, not reality. We can also see the limited ability of those outside the university to determine what this issue actually means. The narrative is powerful. It has initiated government responses and provided the framing for policy action in multiple territories. This matters because it is an external influence that strikes to the heart of the liberal university. We can see the interplay of knowledge and power between those inside the university and those outside it. Who gets to control this agenda matters because it fundamentally affects the teaching mission, influencing what is taught and what sort of learning environment is encouraged on campus. If free speech is a problem, it has to be dealt with in a proportionate and evidence-based way.

3.5 Student Spies and Security

Beneath the headline message of the knowledge economy, which advocates investment in universities, the knowledge economy narrative produces additional imperatives that generate more complex policy problems to be solved. This rests on the idea that national economic competitiveness in a global economy requires the *nation* to maintain a competitive edge over its counterparts. Considering the importance of the application of knowledge to economic success, there is a need for knowledge to be restricted to institutions within the nation state to prevent it from being exploited by rivals first. To maintain the competitive advantage of the nation, policymakers may need to put some regulations in place to restrict the flow of some intellectual property out of the country. One channel by which knowledge can be transferred to other countries is through international students who return home and apply what they have learned.

This long-standing national economic competitiveness argument has been accompanied in the last decade with a growing security one. Rather than universities merely aiding the competitiveness of foreign firms or economies by providing knowledge they can take to market first, the knowledge can be also applied in ways that are detrimental to national security. This takes place at a time when economic and security concerns are increasingly interlinked.

This security concern is illustrated well by the 2018 *Australian Strategic Policy Institute* report *Picking Flowers, Making Honey*. The report documents how since 2007 China's People's Liberation Army (PLA) sponsored more than 2,500 military scientists and engineers to study abroad, with the Five Eyes countries (the United States, United Kingdom, Australia, Canada, and New Zealand) plus Germany and Singapore being the main destinations. The research finds nearly all of these PLA scientists are Chinese Communist Party members who typically conceal their military affiliations when applying to study abroad. These students usually study subjects covering content such as hypersonic missiles and navigation technology. They then return to China on completion of their studies, where it is alleged they apply their knowledge and skills to develop military technology which could, potentially, be used on the rest of the world. In this view, China's goal is to not only catch up but overtake other powers in military technology. There is no reciprocity in this arrangement, as non-Chinese are not allowed to study in certain Chinese institutes, meaning the intellectual benefits flow only one way (Joske, 2018). (Of course, the financial benefits of enrolling foreign students provide an incentive for universities to welcome such individuals.)

This security concern also raises a significant dilemma because these study destinations, which encourage Chinese students to study in their universities, regard China as a main intelligence adversary. The *Australian Strategic Policy Institute* report noted the naivety that has hitherto surrounded this issue: 'helping a rival military develop its expertise and technology isn't in the national interest, yet it's not clear that Western universities and governments are fully aware of this phenomenon'. This Australian-based research notes universities have not self-regulated on this issue and have not controlled the associated security risks, while government policy towards universities working with the PLA has been lacking. The report recommended closer engagement between governments and universities who need to see a distinction between the beneficial and harmful effects of internationalisation. It advised governments to explore a wider range of tools such as better scrutiny of visa applications and further legislation targeting military end users. Interestingly, the report also suggested governments increase funding to strategic science and technology, meaning universities would be less likely to seek income from enrolling foreign students (Joske, 2018).

The dilemma is clear: on the one hand, universities are incentivised to recruit more high-fee-paying international students as they desire the revenue to fund their activities – this includes the cross-subsidisation of research. This aligns with the incentive to perform well in global rankings, as research power and the numbers of international students are both criteria. On the other hand, the state may use its power as the issuer of study visas to restrict entry to certain international students for economic and security reasons. The tension seen here is growing, indicated by the number of countries paying greater attention to foreign student admissions.

This scenario can be seen in the United States, where the number of Chinese international students has grown exponentially. In the late 1970s, before President Carter established formal diplomatic ties that fostered China–US student exchange in 1979, there were fewer than 1,000 Chinese students in the United States. Forty years later in 2019, there were 370,000. However, the Trump administration introduced the *Extreme Visa Vetting Policy* and in 2020 revoked the visas of over 1,000 'high risk' Chinese students (Togoh, 2020). Furthermore, the US Congress addressed concerns that national economic and military security was being undermined by giving foreign governments, particularly China, unfair access to new technology by passing the *Securing American Science and Technology Act of 2019* (Mervis 2019).

New interventions can be seen in the United Kingdom, which further tightened controls in 2021 by expanding the *Academic Technology Approval Scheme*, which checks students and researchers applying for courses with military applications. The government told universities it had to go further in mitigating security risks as there was a 'significant threat to the UK's national and broader global security' (Staton et al., 2021).

In another example, Japan, as a study destination, was seen as a soft target for student spies. This is owing to the lack of relevant anti-espionage law and universities seeking international recruitment in response to domestic demographic pressures flowing from a declining population. Until recently, the Japanese government regarded security and technology as unconnected policy concerns. These have now been united in a new unit of the National Security Secretariat focussed entirely on economic statecraft, operating at the intersection of economic security and national security, which is charged with the protection of sensitive technology (Osaki 2020). The Japanese felt the need to intervene as there are effects of other nations having done so. There is a possibility that students with spying intentions who have been blocked by countries with stricter screening will simply study in Japan if the softer status quo is maintained. The Japanese authorities were also concerned that such a situation would jeopardise military cooperation and joint university-based research with allies and compromise the Quadrilateral Security Dialogue between the United States, Japan, Australia, and India (the Quad) that is leading the Free and Open Indo-Pacific vision that is a response to Chinese assertiveness (Sim, 2020).

Universities are tied, directly or indirectly, to the security interests of the nation state where they are based and to wider geopolitics. As a more uncertain global security situation leads to tighter restrictions, universities may feel their autonomy encroached. For policymakers, this is not an easy problem to address, as it is potentially more complex than simply preventing applicants from one country studying one group of subjects. How governments can protect national economic advantage, maintain security, and restrict knowledge falling into the wrong hands while maintaining the cosmopolitan character of campuses will be challenging (Grubbs, 2019).

3.6 Measuring Teaching

The teaching mission has gained increased attention, and perhaps importance, in recent years. It has also been subject to increased scrutiny, resulting in calls for greater transparency. This has been driven by a range of factors such as the diminishing graduate wage premium and rising student fees, requiring universities to demonstrate 'return on investment' and 'value for money'. The key trend is the growing view that universities need to be more accountable. Assessing teaching quality is challenging. While there is considerable agreement around the definition of research excellence and the indicators that can be used to assess it, much less agreement pertains when considering teaching excellence.

Performance measurement of the teaching mission is often intertwined with the practice of performance-based funding (PBF). The rationales for PBF are well rehearsed amongst policy scholars as such schemes neatly align with NPM thinking. There are some things universities will not do on their own, either effectively or at all, which are social goals or public goods. The role of the state is to establish what these things are and find a way to make them happen. PBF arrangements are useful for the state as a means to get universities to do certain things. Moreover, incentivising with rewards is more a subtle way of treating institutions that enjoy a degree of autonomy than the exercise of directives. The incentives of PBF, when accompanied by performance evaluations that produce performance data, are a useful way for policymakers to both make policy change and monitor its implementation.

There are numerous examples worldwide of policymakers applying PBF models to higher education, and, in recent years, a growing number of empirical studies have investigated the implementation and implications of such schemes. For example, in Ontario, Canada, a PBF model was developed to be used in the province. Here, indicators measure universities' performance by the labour-market and economic outcomes of graduates (Spooner, 2019). This has been criticised as it will move universities 'from being institutions dedicated to fostering critical, creative and engaged citizens that generate public-interest research toward institutions with newly conceived narrow missions' (Spooner, 2021).

PBF has been a popular tool for state lawmakers in the United States (Bell et al., 2018). A study by Kelchen and Stedrak (2016) suggests 'that public colleges that face at least some funding being tied to outcomes do change their expenditure patterns and potentially even the composition of their student body' (p. 317). This study illustrates how the effects can be perverse, such as universities trying to attract more students from higher-income families. Other studies have identified different effects. For example, Rutherford and Rabovsky (2014) find that performance funding policies 'are not associated with higher levels of student performance' and Ortagus et al. (2020) find 'there is also compelling evidence that PBF policies lead to unintended outcomes related to restricting access, gaming of the PBF system, and disadvantages for underserved student groups and under-resourced institution types'.

This identifies the value of policy theory to aiding our understanding of the complex and nuanced effects of a policy intervention. Future social science research, which interrogates how performance funding works, may inform future policy interventions. For example, Mizrahi (2021) develops a theoretical framework with a 'network-related principal agent framework' to identify the possible origins of the failures in many versions of performance funding in higher education. The research finds the conditions required that would make performance funding work rarely exist. This 'ultimately explains the failures in accountability related to performance funding' and calls for 'expanding the collection of performance information to include inputs and capabilities and creating various mechanisms that connect specific solutions to specific problems'.

Policy interventions have also evolved in this area. For example, the United Kingdom moved a step further than having a series of criteria to measure performance that could inform funding. In 2015, the United Kingdom launched an assessment framework designed to serve a wider range of functions and aimed at a wider audience. The *Teaching Excellence Framework* (TEF) illustrates how the state has sought to achieve greater transparency across higher education as well as to incentivise institutional behaviour. National governments insist on greater accountability and transparency to protect the interests of consumers, while in the large global marketplace of university courses, high-fee-paying international students require information to make a choice. In terms of incentives, the United Kingdom government introduced the TEF as a way of raising esteem for teaching; recognising and rewarding excellent teaching; and getting universities to better meet the needs of employers, business, industry, and the professions.

The TEF differs from other performance funding schemes with respect to both how performance is evaluated and how it was intended to inform funding. The TEF is a multi-variable framework that combines both metrics and judgement of a panel of peers. The framework assesses teaching quality (through student satisfaction), learning environment, and student/graduate outcomes. The developmental work of the TEF – which involved designing both institutional and subject-level assessments and whole new metrics – illustrates the unprecedented scale of the scheme as a performance evaluation framework for the teaching mission. How the TEF was designed to determine funding was also complex. The reward for universities with a high TEF score, as the scheme was originally intended, was permission to charge high fees to domestic students who are in the public system of fees and loans, although this was later dropped. The main funding reward comes indirectly, in the form of intangible assets – such as reputation, attention, legitimacy, certified quality – that flow from a high score, from which universities can then recruit more students and raise more money (Gunn 2018a, 2018b). In the five years following its introduction, the TEF was subject to considerable development and refinement. This can be attributed to the experimental nature of the scheme; some aspects of it worked, while others did not. These changes highlight the considerable operational difficulties when developing a metric-driven performance framework for the teaching mission (see Gunn, 2022).

3.7 Conclusion

In this section, we noted how the teaching mission incorporates the inputs, processes, outputs, and outcomes of the whole student life cycle. Various contemporary challenges have emerged relating to these activities; driven by factors such as globalisation, new technologies, and governments seeking greater accountability. The key message to take from this section is how the teaching mission is about far more than different approaches to pedagogy. It is situated in a complex context involving a wider range of issues, such as protecting national security and enhancing human capital. The role of context is particularly evident when wider societal and political issues spill over into campus life – recent debates on free speech being a pertinent example. Issues such as these can be advanced by advocacy coalitions outside the academic community who successfully use narratives and framing to raise the profile of their cause. This has resulted in political leaders paying more attention to what happens on campuses; and various legislative moves across multiple countries have seen governments seeking to exercise more control over what can, and cannot, happen in university teaching spaces, laboratories, and student union buildings.

4 The Research Mission of the University

4.1 Introduction

When the public think about universities, they usually think about people earning degrees. As the teaching mission of the university is the most salient in society, politicians tend to focus their attention on issues including how many people go to university and how it is paid for, or the employability of graduates. Research, therefore, gets much less public and political attention; although there are exceptions when scientific breakthroughs occur that may save lives. However, for academics employed in universities, the research mission is by far the most salient. It is worth briefly exploring the peculiar relationship between these two missions.

The long-standing tension between the university as a place of teaching and as a place of research endures because time and resources are finite. University leaders know that high-quality research is vital for raising the overall status of their institutions, and such status is essential for attracting quality and high-fee-paying students in sufficient quantity. But they also know that teaching must be taken seriously. This is the service people are paying for. University leaders want their alumni to look back favourably on their alma mater. This same basic tension exists at the operational level in each department. Students bring in the money, but research generates academic prestige. Individual academics often seek to be highly effective teachers. Yet, they also recognise that time spent on teaching reduces the attention they can give to research. And for the purpose of securing employment, gaining promotions, and remaining competitive in the academic job market, evidence of research quality and income generation are almost always more valuable than evidence of exceptional teaching performance.

In this section, we discuss the rise and consolidation of the research university. Having reviewed this broader context, we discuss the potential for political influence to shape the research mission in universities. We then consider how states steer research through funding and evaluation mechanisms.

4.2 Key Elements of the Research Process

Although teaching is critical to the transmission of knowledge, the general advancement of knowledge comes through research-based acts of discovery.

This is why the research mission matters and it is this that distinguishes the university from all other teaching institutions. Research can be problem-directed, responding to an issue in society or one presented by a funder. Research efforts can also be curiosity-driven, motivated primarily by the interests of researchers who might gain their inspiration from a variety of questions or puzzles, and who approach their research using concepts and methods that represent the accumulation of knowledge in their given disciplines (Strandburg, 2005).

We can delineate the research mission of the university by focussing on four components: research inputs, environment, research outputs and by-products, and product and service development. Inputs include knowledge-able people, formal and informal rules of conduct, and physical resources. Funding, as an essential input, is the focus of Sections 4.5 and 4.6. The combination of these inputs determines the research environment. Research outputs are typically publications; even when outputs come in other forms – such as inventions, computer programs, medical devices, or new materials – it is often the case that their production has been documented in a publication. Research can also generate other things. These include: first, the development of the skills, knowledge, and networks of the researchers involved, which all contribute to institutional capacity; second, the development of new knowledge to be deployed in the teaching mission and elsewhere; and third, increasing stakeholder perceptions of the whole university (i.e. there are reputational effects that can be used to leverage future resources).

4.3 The Rise of the Research University

While universities have existed for centuries as distinctive organisational entities, the research university is a comparatively recent phenomenon. The rise of the research university is credited with the transformations of universities and the employment arrangements for academics in nineteenth-century Germany (O'Boyle, 1983). The distinctive feature of the German model was that academic staff gained positions and promotions based on the quality of their research. This led to a flourishing of research activity on campus. The belief also emerged during this period that effective teaching in the university and production of quality research were complementary activities. All academic staff were encouraged to engage in both original research and teaching. Doctoral studies were treated as the fundamental research-based path by which people could enter the academic profession. German universities professionalised early because German society was bureaucratic. As English and American societies became more complex and required more trained experts, their universities began to emulate the German model (Menand et al., 2017).

In the United States, the German model of the university was first emulated explicitly with the development of Johns Hopkins University (founded in 1876) and the University of Chicago (founded in 1890). Among the emerging public universities, the University of Michigan (founded in 1817) also came to deliberately forge a path that was styled after the research-oriented German universities. While the first two presidents of the University of Michigan had this ambition, it was the third president, James B. Angell (who served in the role from 1871 to 1909), who brought it to fruition. As universities emulating the German model gained prestige and influence, others began to consciously follow. Consequently, in the later nineteenth century, long-established universities such as Harvard and Yale in the United States and Oxford and Cambridge in the United Kingdom underwent major transformations to reposition themselves from finishing schools for the elite to leading research institutions. Although there has been considerable variation, the institutional isomorphism producing research universities is notable for how striking and enduring it is. The rise of the research university is a classic illustration of historical institutionalism and the diffusion of innovations through a set of ideas travelling across different jurisdictions.

Although this model was enduring, it would not remain static in perpetuity. It would of course evolve. In the 2000s scholars began documenting changes to the research university. For example, Baker (2007, 2008) observed the advent of the 'super research university' that came to fruition towards the end of the twentieth century, after decades of incremental change in the United States. There were 'a small but growing number of these institutions . . . able to produce unprecedented levels of science, technology, and knowledge about human society'. Mohrman et al. (2008) define eight characteristics of what they call 'The Emerging Global Model'. These universities exhibit: (1) a global perspective that transcends the boundaries of the nation state, (2) a research-intensive focus, (3) academics taking on new roles with more research taking place in international partnerships directed towards real-world problems, (4) a diversified funding based to finance their expensive research enterprise, (5) the forging of new relationships with governments and corporations to advance economic development and the social good, (6) worldwide recruitment strategies for students and staff, (7) complex internal organisation such as interdisciplinary centres, and (8) global networking activities that support collaborative research, student and faculty mobility, and validation of international stature.

We see here the evolution of the elite research university in the context of globalisation. It is worth noting two features of super universities that Baker observed from the vantage point of the 2000s. First, as high-cost operations they tend to be financed by private money and many are privately controlled. Second, they are 'not the product of some central plan' but rather 'grew out of a unique set of historical conditions' during the massification of US higher education, where large sums of money were being channelled into the sector (Baker, 2008, p. 46). As this model took hold, governments promoted this model of the university through policy interventions and by using public money to create new flagship institutions. We explore these wider institutional transformations in Section 6.

In discussing the Emerging Global Model, Mohrman et al. (2008) note how the worldwide reach of these institutions 'means that nation-states have less influence over their universities than in the past'. To what extent this is true, and how the influence has changed, needs to be subject to ongoing policy research. It must be remembered that these elite universities are not most universities. Even within particular jurisdictions, universities differ in the emphasis they place on research versus teaching. However, the attributes of this model illustrate some of the changes that have taken place in the research mission more broadly, which are explored next.

4.4 Changing Contexts

Marginson (2021) observes that following the arrival of the Internet a growth and diversification of capacity and output in science has pushed a shift from science being produced and organised solely in national systems to the emergence of a 'distinctive global science system'. This is driven by flat, open networked relations combined with the inequalities produced by global hegemony that are arbitrarily modified by national governments and specific resources. At the level of the researcher, another trend has seen the massive increase in the volume of material being published, known as the 'publish or perish' culture that has affected research practice, often adversely (see Moosa, 2018, p. 173–176). The geopolitics of science is also in flux. Brenner (2018) describes a situation where:

> The global dominance of the United States of America has been partially broken ... Europe is in the process of forming a coherent continental knowledge policy but with considerable constraints, while China, and many other Asian nations, are mobilizing knowledge in the pursuit of societal modernization, organized in various forms of authoritarian governance. Some significant parts of the world remain marginal in the global circulation of knowledge; but they too aim to be part of the 'new global politics of research' (Benner, 2018, p. 177).

A significant change has been the rise of China as 'the biggest scientific powerhouse in the Asia Pacific region' (Nguyen and Choung, 2020). A landmark was reached when China was declared the world's largest producer of scientific articles (Tollefson, 2018), in a move Basu et al. (2018) saw as 'China merely regaining its historical position of leadership in science and technology'.

These things matter to governments as the knowledge economy narrative situates states, their universities and the scientific endeavours pursued within them as competitors in a 'global race'. University rankings have grown in prominence as they meet the demand for 'scorecards' on this 'race'. This is despite the flaws and limitations of ranking systems identified by academic researchers (Lim, 2018). Although different rankings use different methodologies, the most followed rankings – *the Academic Ranking of World Universities, Quacquarelli Symonds World University Rankings, Times Higher Education World University Rankings*, and *the CWTS Leiden Ranking* – are mostly measuring the research mission (Moed, 2017). This means a whole university can be judged on research performance alone, highlighting the importance of the research mission.

Rankings are not just of interest to commentators, universities, and prospective students. They are of interest to policymakers too. As Hazelkorn (2018) notes: 'We are accustomed with the way in which governments have unashamedly used rankings to re-shape strategy, systems and resource allocation.' The rationale for rankings has, therefore, become part of the framing for research policy; and as these are world rankings and competition is global we can see this trend diffuse worldwide.

Another trend in research policy has been the growth in massive government-funded programmes to bolster national scientific and economic performance, such as the *European Research Council*, which was launched by the EU in 2007 to fund basic research in the bloc (König, 2017). In the context of greater competition, Japan announced in 2021 the new University Fund, which according to projections would involve a total spend of JP¥10 trillion, making it one of world's largest science endowment funds. The stated reason is to restore Japan's standing in the international rankings and close the funding gap between its universities and their international peers. Japanese policymakers were responding to the country falling from 4th to 11th in the world in the number of top-level academic papers published over the last two decades. Endowments remain smaller than the United States: Japan's wealthiest private institution, Keio University, possesses a ¥73 billion endowment, which is small compared to Harvard University's which equates to roughly ¥4.5 trillion (Takeo and Urabe, 2021). This move follows a succession of government interventions – such as greater resource concentration in leading institutions and the use of competitive research funding – to address the relative decline of Japanese universities since the 1990s (Yonezawa et al., 2020). The Japanese example shows how nurturing elite research universities can involve the state layering different policy interventions over time, to initiate structural change or improve researcher productivity, in the face of rising regional competitors.

4.5 Political Influence

Basic, pure, or blue skies research is important because there is often a degree of serendipity to the process of discovery. Research discoveries cannot be foreseen and therefore cannot be planned by the state. However, the burden of funding pure research typically falls upon the state because the corporate world tends to not fund activities that produce no immediate return, that is, pure research is a textbook example of a public good. And, as with all public goods, incentives exist for all to freeride on the actions of others, and this can lead to limited or no funding of pure research in the absence of government provision. In this section, we consider how the state operates within this scenario.

As the primary funders of basic research, the state holds the power to steer academic research in numerous ways, with varying degrees of intrusiveness. While the precise arrangements vary between jurisdictions, the vast majority of universities rely heavily on governments to fund research. We can see in the United States – apart from tiny but salient collection of private universities, exemplified by the Ivy League – research universities have always been shaped by government policies. This has occurred because these universities have long been beholden to governments for financial support. In addition to drawing from a portion of student fee income, research may also be funded by business and philanthropic sources. High-profile examples of this could be said to undercut this claim about the powerful influence of government on research universities. However, we suggest that this high profile has resulted precisely because those examples of private funding for research are relatively uncommon.

Political influence on the research mission tends to not draw public attention as it manifests itself mostly through budgetary processes. In the United States, university research spending experienced a significant boost during the Second World War, but that boost was deliberately hidden from public view. From 1941 through to 1945, the Manhattan Project that produced the atomic bombs used on Hiroshima and Nagasaki operated across multiple sites, including Columbia University, the University of Chicago, and the University of California – Berkeley. During this period, the federal government's contribution to funding of research jumped more than tenfold and came to account for over 80 per cent of total science spending in the United

States. This set the scene for subsequent development of the National Science Foundation and the consolidation of the National Institutes. In a report to the president completed in 1944, *Science: The Endless Frontier*, Vannevar Bush set forth three principles to guide public research funding in the United States. The first was that research grants should be made directly to universities. The second was that nonpartisan experts should be relied upon to select the projects to be funded, and there should be no political interference in the conduct of research. The third was that funding should be channelled through institutions operating at arm's length from government and that funding should be stable and predictable over time. The first two principles have subsequently guided research funding. The third was not adopted. In the United States, government funding of research continues to be channelled through a range of government agencies. That funding is often subject to tough budgetary decision-making, whereby research funding for universities waxes and wanes. The creation in the United States of this competitive extramural system for funding research has been widely emulated around the world.

Political influence on the research mission of universities rarely stretches to the level of details concerning specific research projects. Exceptions tend to relate to the funding of research projects in the humanities where politicians demure over taxes being used to fund seemingly prurient, profane, or obscure activities. For example, a controversy caused in the late 1980s by the work of American artist and photographer Andres Serrano, whose work had been funded from the National Endowment for the Arts, led to subsequent budget cuts to the Endowment. Also in the United States, in May 2012, Representative Jeff Flake (R-AZ) attempted to eliminate political science funding from the National Science Foundation (NSF) budget. This was the third time since 1995 that Republicans in Congress attempted to cut NSF funding for political science (Uscinski and Klofstad, 2013).

In Australia, controversy arose in 2018 when an education minister blocked funding of eleven grants in the humanities approved by the Australian Research Council. The Senator at the centre of the controversy, Simon Birmingham, said, 'I make no apologies for ensuring that taxpayer research dollars weren't spent on projects that Australians would rightly view as being entirely wrong priorities.' The chief executive of Universities Australia, a peak body, retorted that 'You don't expect the federal sports minister to choose Australia's Olympic team. In the same way, we rely on subject experts to judge the best research in their field, not politicians' (Universities Australia, 2018). This ministerial veto power over research funding allocations has been a source of on-going controversy in Australia.

Academic research can be politically controversial resulting in political interference. Human embryonic stem cell research is an area where political choices have explicitly influenced public funding of university-based research. Interestingly, those political choices have differed significantly across jurisdictions (Rewerski, 2007). The result has been that some jurisdictions have come to be seen as much more conducive environments for conducting stem cell research than others. In the United States, federal government funding of this research was circumscribed when, in 2001, President George W. Bush set forth clear guidelines on the use of human embryonic stem cells in any research funded by the US government. The state of California subsequently stole a march on such research when a citizen ballot initiative opened the way for creation of a stem cell research agency funded by state government sources outside the control of the state legislature. This represented an unusual case of clearly made political arguments shaping the funding of research that was conducted principally in research universities (Mintrom, 2009b). The case also illustrated the influence that advocacy coalitions can have on public policy relating to permissible research and government funding for it. States with strong research capacity in this area were more likely to maintain support for stem cell research. In contrast, the states where it was banned tended to have governments influenced by conservative Christians. But those states also tended to lack strengths in the biological sciences. In that sense, the bans on stem cell research in certain states could be rightly construed as grandstanding, since very little stem cell research was likely to have ever been conducted at universities within their borders in any case. However, this illustrates how actions of advocacy coalitions contribute to cross-jurisdictional differences in science policies. Political conditions in a given jurisdiction can determine what advocacy coalitions may emerge and whether they are successful in securing policy change, which can determine what areas of research are funded or even permitted.

4.6 Research Evaluation

Typically state involvement is not as direct as in the examples mentioned previously. Rather it is more continuous and indirect, achieved through designing the mechanisms that distribute the money that unleash incentives and change behaviour. Here, performance-based research funding systems (PRFSs) determine the allocation of government funds to universities on the basis of ex-post assessments of research performance (Geuna and Martin, 2003; Ochsner et al., 2020). The first such scheme was the UK *Research Assessment Exercise* (RAE), which was piloted in 1986 and subsequently replaced by the

Research Excellence Framework (REF). The evolution of this scheme illustrates how policymakers refine PRFSs over time. Considering the effects of the RAE/REF, Nixon (2020) argues they 'created a new and increasingly dominant order' that has 'impacted on the mind-set of academic practitioners by defining the norms of academic professionalism and academic practice. A new kind of orderliness now circumscribes and defines what it means to be an academic' (p. 11–12).

Providing a noteworthy example of policy transfer, the RAE was widely emulated internationally; by 2010, fourteen other countries had launched comparable schemes. These include Italy's *Valutazione della qualità della ricerca* (VQR) (Grisorio and Prota, 2020) and Australia's *Excellence in Research for Australia* (ERA) (Martin-Sardesai et al., 2019). Thomas et al. (2020) argue PRFSs 'are becoming the predominant means worldwide to allocate research funds and accrue reputation for universities', indicating there may be continuing policy convergence. Hicks (2012) finds the powerful incentives created within university systems by PRFSs have driven public competition for prestige more than the redistribution of funding. This is a reminder that PRFSs are like rankings, that is, they create reputational rewards. PRFSs have been viewed by academics as an encroachment into their independence; however, when looking at the effects of PRFSs on institutional autonomy, Hicks (2012) finds the evidence is ambiguous, and in some circumstances, PRFSs enhance the control of professional elites.

Today, governments go to considerable lengths to assess the research being produced in universities. This development has two key sources. First, the recognition that resources are finite and funds spent on university-based research could potentially yield higher gains to society if they were deployed elsewhere. We see here how PRFSs flow neatly from the NPM agenda. Second, the recognition that universities generate research-based knowledge of value to society. But this raises the question of how good is the research being produced? In setting the rules for research evaluation, policymakers need to resist the temptation to impose excessive accountability systems or to micromanage research practices. Governments should support basic research through sound and stable funding programmes. They should avoid sending mixed signals to researchers and universities.

A significant trend in research evaluation has been the shift from judgement to metrics. Hicks et al. (2015) note that 'evaluations that were once bespoke and performed by peers are now routine and reliant on metrics', which 'risks damaging the system with the very tools designed to improve it'. This is because metrics can be 'gamed' (Biagioli and Lippman, 2020). For example, studies show academic publishing metrics have become targets and follow Goodhart's Law, according to which, 'when a measure becomes a target, it ceases to be a good measure' (Fire and Guestrin, 2019). If metrics are incorporated into PRFSs, this should be done responsibly (Wilsdon et al., 2015).

Although these schemes may have common rationales, they differ considerably. For example, a study of PRFSs in the EU by Zacharewicz et al. (2019) found major variations in the assessments that feed into the funding allocation formula. The authors noted that even within the two main types of assessments (metrics-based and peer review-based) the approaches adopted varied. This range of different assessments illustrates the large amount of discretion policymakers have when designing them. And into this space, policymakers bring value judgements. A study by Pinar (2020) regarding the funding formula used by Research England revealed the money universities receive not only depends on the quality of research activity carried out but also on the value judgement of policymakers that manifest themselves within the formula, such as weightings by subject costs and research rating.

Recent research shows that state research funding choices produce a range of ramifications at different levels. First, competitive funding streams can influence publishing patterns. For example, a comparative study by Wang et al. (2020) into the effect of competitive public funding on China and the EU found that funding agencies play a key role in influencing research behaviour. It concluded that the Chinese arrangements produce a high number of publications. In contrast, the EU's schemes place more focus on social impact, and the EU funding schemes are also tools to promote European integration. Second, public funding can influence institutional performance. Research by Benito et al. (2019) investigated the influence of public funding on the position reached by the top 300 universities in the *Quaccarelly Symond World University Ranking* 2018. The analysis reveals that public funding was critical in explaining the placing of 84 per cent of the top universities, particularly the European ones. The study also showed the top 100 universities had double the level of funding compared to those ranked 101–200 and triple that of universities in positions 201–300. This finding reaffirmed the notion that the highest-ranked universities are usually the best resourced. Third, the design of government-funding schemes can influence international collaboration, an increasingly important part of the research process. Zhou et al. (2020) undertook a study into the different arrangements of funding agencies in six developing and developed countries and internationally collaborated publications. The research found international collaboration improves citation impact, with developing countries benefitting more.

4.7 Conclusion

In this section, we reviewed the rise of the research university and detailed the emergence of a single global model for the elite research university. In the process, we noted how governments have increasingly come to recognise the strategic value of universities. The role of the funder empowers the state to exercise power over the production of knowledge in various ways. We can see this presents potential opportunities for the politicisation of science. Moreover, in evaluating academic research the state is able to set the institutional 'rules of the game' (as introduced in Section 2.2) for researchers in a given jurisdiction. The trend towards measuring return on investment from public spending and the rise of global university rankings have served to raise the pressure on universities and their researchers to demonstrate their excellence. The globalisation of science, combined with the high degree of policy transfer between states in how research is evaluated and funded, has resulted in greater international convergence in the organisation and focus of research activities in the contemporary university.

5 The Third Mission of the University

5.1 Introduction

The third mission of the university is a catch-all term relating to the social, enterprise, and innovation activities beyond teaching and research that bring the university into direct contact with society. The notion of a third mission is based on a linear account of the evolution of the university, where the institution is seen as having emerged as a place of teaching and then research. Referring to this mission by its ordinal form, rather than by an activity, gives the classification generic longevity, placing it above the ever-evolving range of activities that fall within it. The third mission builds on the university's powerful claim to distinction as a means for both imparting knowledge through teaching and generating new knowledge through research. The third mission represents a concerted effort to bring the university into direct engagement with select stakeholders. In the process, it highlights the contribution the university makes to society for those who might otherwise remain oblivious to the role universities play in advancing the good society and knowledge-based prosperity.

The university is often portrayed as an 'ivory tower' – an institution that stands at a distance from society. The ivory tower, we are told, is aloof. It exhibits a certain disdain or disregard for events of the day and practical affairs. This puts the university out of the loop of business, worldly affairs, and politics. As with all caricature, there is a certain degree of truth in this account.

Historically, many universities were deliberately situated outside of the city limits, with the intent of removing scholars from the many temptations and distractions that cities present. And, indeed, serious study can require lengthy periods of quiet, calm, focus, and reflection. Organisational environments need to be carefully designed and managed to promote conducive conditions for academic work. To appropriate Daniel Kahneman's (2012) distinction between fast and slow thinking in the human mind, we might say that both learning and research call for dedication to slow thinking. Slow thinking in support of knowledge generation requires removal of distractions. Consequently, researchers must establish suitable filters to keep at bay the noise and clamour characteristic of much public life.

Meanwhile, there's 'the real world'. No matter how we construe it, the world outside of the university is continuously encountering challenges, problems, and dilemmas that call for investigation and for the development of effective responses. It would seem reasonable to expect universities to lend their sub-stantial capabilities to address the urgent matters societies face. Further, all universities – be they public or private – operate on funding that derives from real-world activities. As we saw in Section 4, universities derive some of their funding from government sources and this comes with growing expectations. It is no surprise that politicians and other influential figures periodically voice a desire for universities to be more visibly engaged in society. This tension between 'the ivory tower' and 'the real world' gives rise to much of the interplay between knowledge and power.

This section is structured as follows. Section 5.2 considers developments in the United States, which illustrate how universities have long been engaged with the world around them and how this has changed over time. The United States is a noteworthy case as it produced examples other nations sought to emulate. Section 5.3 explains how the third mission developed to arrive at its present form. The key elements of this mission are then unpacked in Section 5.4 followed by a look at the role of government intervention in Section 5.5. We then consider in Section 5.6 how this mission can be measured.

5.2 The US Experience

Universities have always been connected to the political and economic contexts around them. The history of US higher education provides a case study of this, which also illustrates the role of lawmakers. The land-grant universities were established in the United States under the Morrill Acts of 1862 and 1890. The American Civil War was raging at the time Congress passed the first of these acts. The Act of 1862 was introduced into Congress by Justin Smith Morrill, a senator from Vermont and was signed into law by President Abraham Lincoln. The Act made provision for federally owned public lands to be donated 'to each loyal state to support a college where the leading object shall be, without excluding other scientific and classical studies and including military tactics, to teach such branches of learning as are related to agriculture and the mechanical arts ... in order to promote the liberal and practical education of the industrial classes in the several pursuits and professions of life'.

There was precedent for this policy initiative. During the 1850s, significant efforts were made in Midwestern states to promote the creation of agricultural colleges. In Michigan, the state constitution adopted in 1850 made provision for such an entity. This resulted in the establishment of an agricultural college in 1855, which evolved into the entity known since 1964 as Michigan State University. That early agricultural college served as the prototype for the entire land-grant system. Today, Michigan State University still proudly refers to itself as the pioneer land-grant university. It maintains its founding role through significant 'outreach' activities that are tightly braided into its research and teaching activities. Other notable land-grant universities include the University of California – Berkeley, the University of Minnesota, Cornell University, and the Massachusetts Institute of Technology (MIT). The Act of 1890 served to extend the land-grant system in the post–Civil War period. Most notably, it prohibited the distribution of money to states that made distinctions of race in admissions unless at least one land-grant university for African Americans was established within the state. So the Act of 1890 promulgated the creation of the historically Black universities in southern states (James, 1910).

There are currently seventy-six land-grant universities in the United States. Their presence offers a powerful reminder of the recognition given early in the history of the nation to knowledge as a key to economic and social development. The earliest land-grant universities placed engagement at the very heart of their operations and forged seamless connections between that outward-facing mission and their teaching mission (McDowell, 2003). The emphasis on intensive production of original research emerged later in their development. This is a reminder that not all universities and jurisdictions neatly fit the order of the three missions model.

Moving into the twentieth century the United States provides us with another set of developments worthy of note. The funding of science projects by the US government in pursuit of military superiority has been credited for the massive economic development around Route 128 in Massachusetts and Silicon Valley in California (Saxenian, 1996). The economic development has yet to abate. As early as the 1950s, the lessons of how university-related research and technology initiatives could stimulate wider economic development were not lost on other regions of the United States. For example, efforts to establish state-subsidised laboratories in what came to be known as the Research Triangle Park in North Carolina had the intended effect of attracting federal research laboratories in the area (Luger, 1991). Today, the Research Triangle contains the highest concentration of people with PhDs within the United States.

During the 1960s and 1970s, these developments in specific regions of the United States led politicians elsewhere to explore how they could bring more benefits of this kind to the jurisdictions they represented (Bayma, 1979). This led to the realisation that the potential for scientific knowledge to be translated into commercial technologies was not being effectively harnessed. At that time, the US federal government held the intellectual property on any federally funded research. Critics expressed the view that a transfer of intellectual property rights could prompt considerably more translation of science findings into usable technologies. This led to the adoption of the Bayh–Dole Act, or the *Patent and Trademark Law Amendments Act of 1980*, which allowed universities, small businesses, and non-profit institutions to maintain ownership of inventions derived from federally funded science projects conducted on site. This act has had important consequences.

Since passage of the Bayh–Dole Act in 1980, universities in the United States have greatly expanded their patenting and licensing activities (Mowery et al., 2015). Analysts observing this change have credited it with having stimulated significant economic growth (Branscomb and Keller, 1998). Others have proposed that considerably more opportunities exist for promoting research-based innovation in the United States, as long as the policy settings are carefully designed. Richard L. Florida has been at the forefront of efforts to explain and promote the ways that university-based scientific inquiry, and the broader culture of technology, talent, and tolerance that surrounds universities, can serve to generate strong local, state, and national economic development (Florida, 2002, 2005). AnnaLee Saxanian's (1996, 2007) studies of regional advantage illustrate the anchoring role that universities can play in creating highly productive relationships that support technological development. In turn, the resulting social and professional networks can generate a form of social capital that facilitates ease of commercial interaction and creation of technology start-ups. Many opportunities appear to exist for universities to strengthen the ties they have with governments at all levels, with the intention of both enhancing university revenue streams and creating opportunities for research to contribute directly to addressing public problems. As William McMillen (2010) observed in *From Campus to Capitol: The Role of Government Relations in Higher Education*, partnerships between universities, government, and industry became more important. This resulted in a sharp increase in the creation of government relations offices on campuses across the United States. Over the past fifty years, a cohort of functional intermediaries has emerged to ensure that universities maintain effective presence in and around policymaking circles. University leadership has come to appreciate the benefits that can flow from continuous engagement with government. When universities work to maintain their salience with government, it makes it easier for them to apply appropriate pressure in the right places when specific benefits are being sought (Bok, 1982; Rhodes, 2001).

5.3 Evolution of the Third Mission

The US example shows engagement is long-standing, yet it has changed. To explain this evolution over time, Rosli and Rossi (2016) present three categories: technology transfer, knowledge transfer, and knowledge exchange. Following the United States, incursions into the third mission in Europe and the United Kingdom began with a focus on promoting *technology transfer.* The arguments made to justify this bore close resemblance to those that led to adoption of the Bayh–Dole Act. That argument suggested universities are repositories of significant research-based knowledge that could readily inform technology development in industry, hence advancing the development of knowledge economies. Consistent with this argument, governments began to create incentives for universities to develop partnerships with industry (Rosli and Rossi, 2016). These incentives often centred on the clarification of intellectual property rights, in a fashion reminiscent of how the Bayh–Dole Act assigned intellectual property rights to US universities for knowledge created through federally funded research grants. Further, efforts encouraged universities to establish spin-off companies and technology parks. Again, this development exhibited significant lesson-drawing from developments that had long been underway in the United States. University efforts to establish technology transfer offices have sometimes been interpreted as the bedrock of what is commonly called 'the entrepreneurial university' (Clark, 1998).

While technology transfer can generate benefits for universities and industry, the limits of the strategy became apparent. For example, beyond the technology transfer offices at Stanford University and MIT, it has long been observed that most technology transfer offices are not major revenue sources for their host universities. Typically, a small number of lucrative patents account for the preponderance of revenues (Kenney and Patton, 2009; Holgersson and Aaboen, 2019). As this tendency became apparent to those promoting the third mission, attention turned to ways of diversifying opportunities for university engagement and revenue generation. For example, in the UK's *Lambert*

Review (HM Treasury, 2003), a broader view was taken of third mission activities, which recognised that universities could contribute much more to society than a narrow set of financially motivated engagements built around patenting. The shift in emphasis from *technology transfer* to *knowledge transfer* saw the third mission expand to include the full range of disciplines in the university. This phase saw developments such as spin-off company creation, the growth of research and development networks with industry partners, the development of new educational products, such as executive education, and the nurturing of complementary businesses (Bekkers and Bodas, 2008). Warwick University's ventures into conference facilities management and provision of commercially based academic recruitment services offer examples of this sort.

This creative expansion of thought and action concerning university engagement in society and the economy has led to a recent view that the third mission exemplifies more than technology or knowledge transfer and is more akin to *knowledge exchange*. This expansive view situates the university as a node within a variety of commercial and non-commercial networks. The 'knowledge exchange' construal of the third mission emphasises the two-way, collaborative nature of interactions between universities and partners in industry and society (Rosli and Rossi, 2016). While potentially amorphous, the knowledge exchange perspective is helpful for making salient the significant capabilities that universities bring to the communities and regions that surround them.

The third mission has grown in importance and scale over time (Knudsen et al., 2021). The notion of the 'engaged' university has become global, with evidence emerging of universities in many countries actively seeking to be more visible contributors to positive social, economic, and environmental outcomes (Compagnucci and Spigarelli, 2020). At an operational level, third-mission endeavours have moved from being 'bottom up' and 'ad hoc' activities of a few entrepreneurial academics to become more 'formalised' and 'institutionalised' (Geuna and Muscio, 2009; Pinheiro et al., 2015). This accounts for why the third mission receives a dedicated section in this Element and why we think it should receive greater attention from policy scholars.

There are two developments that explain why the third mission has developed to take the form it has. First, changing approaches to public management. In addition to the application of NPM reforms, more recently there has been a discernible shift in interest from *output* to *outcome* measurement in government (Newcomer, 2015; Borgonovi et al., 2018). This means organisations in receipt of public money are increasingly expected by the state to demonstrate how they contribute to positive societal outcomes, rather than merely produce data on their outputs. For organisations such as universities, this constitutes a new phase in the accountability agenda when they have to show their worth to achieve external legitimacy and public support. For universities, it is the activities of their third mission that engage with the wider world and therefore deliver the societal outcomes. Here, we can see that as outcomes became more important in how governments judge institutional performance, third-mission activities grew in importance.

Changing ideas on innovation provide a second explanation for why the third mission has developed the way it has. These changes have challenged the traditional linear model. That is to say, they have rejected the assumption of a single starting point of research and an end point of the economy and that the connections happen by themselves. New models have appeared where innovation is seen as decidedly a non-linear process, such as National Innovation Systems (Van der Steen and Enders, 2008). Another such model is the Triple Helix, which comes from the observation that the three previously isolated spheres of university, government, and industry have become increasingly intertwined (Leydesdorff and Etzkowitz, 1996; Etzkowitz and Zhou, 2017). Models such as this place the university 'inside' the innovation system as an integral component part. The role of the university should no longer be viewed as pushing out research into a linear process where the application takes place elsewhere. Rather, *exchange* occurs, where the impetus for innovation is as likely to exist outside the university as inside it. Placing universities inside the innovation system has provided a rationale to develop a plethora of third mission activities to house the interactions – with firms, research users, and so on – needed to make innovation occur. The state often plays a role in driving this process through innovation policy interventions. That is because having the optimal innovation arrangements is seen as essential for achieving economic competitiveness in the global knowledge economy. This trend is evident in a diverse range of economies (see Krishna, 2017; Gaofeng et al., 2021).

5.4 Key Elements of the Third Mission

The diversity of the modern university means the total range of external engagements is considerable. The activities of the third mission are highly heterogeneous and cannot be stereotyped. For example, because some third mission activities have been pursued by universities to develop additional income streams, there is a perception this mission is about making money. This is not entirely true. As we saw in Section 5.3, patents and licensing generate little revenue for most universities. Moreover, many third mission activities – such as civic engagement with local communities, NGOs, or charities – present limited opportunities to generate income. The same is true for academics who may be collaborating with a government department to improve public service delivery. For this reason, some third mission activities are sometimes subsidised by the two classical missions of teaching and research. However, some activities – such as spin-offs – are more closely aligned with profit-seeking firms, and there may be scope for income generation. Indeed, it is clear some operations – such as science parks, technology transfer offices, and incubators – are part of the innovation infrastructure.

It must also be understood that there is considerable overlap between the third mission and the other two missions. The introduction to this section sets up the 'real-world' engagement of the third mission as being the antithesis of the quiet reflection of the 'ivory tower'. In practice, the two are not always in conflict. Third mission activities can strengthen the two classical missions (Vorley and Nelles, 2008), which explains why some call for as much integration as possible (Goddard et al., 2016). For example, where enterprise and entrepreneurial education lead to activities such as the launching of graduate start-up businesses, we can see the teaching and third missions meeting in a mutually beneficial way. Moreover, practitioners outside of the university also generate knowledge, and access to that knowledge can be salutary for guiding research. Donald E. Stokes (1997) observed this salutary aspect of engagement, finding that applied research projects can often present challenges that force researchers back to conducting blue skies research.

Contemporary third mission activities often highlight how creative and engaged academics can forge alliances across organisational boundaries. These boundary spanners can be entrepreneurial in the sense of generating new opportunities for the application of knowledge. They can also do much to advance local political support for universities. In that sense, they can be seen as assisting university leaders in the essential work of building and maintaining the advocacy coalitions that are necessary to ensure scarce public and private resources keep flowing into university coffers.

5.5 Market Failure and Government Intervention

Using the economics literature, Kochenkova et al. (2016) identify four 'market inefficiencies' that provide the rationale for state interventions to support universities' third mission. These barriers are: first a *funding gap*, as university-generated inventions tend to be embryonic in nature they carry considerable risks in terms of any future commercialisation; second, *systemic failure*, where the various players do not effectively interact because of a lack of incentives for collaborations between organisations at different stages of the innovation process; third, *communication gaps*, such as poor comprehension of academic principles and culture by industry and vice versa; and fourth, *knowledge gaps*, where academics and entrepreneurs might lack the managerial competences to move their ideas to a point where they can negotiate with industrial partners.

Government intervention is typically not restricted to addressing these issues and can be more wide ranging. In a study of technology transfer policies, Guerrero and Urbano (2019) identify five types of intervention: the supply side (direct funding for research and development, fiscal measures, debt schemes, technology services), the demand side (innovation procurement schemes), connectivity (clusters), regulatory frameworks (intellectual property rights), as well as complementary frameworks (financing, market, labour).

A striking area of policy convergence, particular in Europe, can be seen in the abolition of the long-standing 'Professor's Privilege' – where university researchers retain ownership of academic inventions – and its replacement with a Bayh–Dole Act arrangement where intellectual property belongs to the employing institution. Gores and Link (2021) call this the *Globalization of the Bayh–Dole Act* and argue that the Act's most overlooked effect has been its influence on policy in other countries. The authors also note that Bayh–Dole-like policies have been more effective in some countries than in others. This corresponds with other research that finds moving to the university ownership model is not a panacea and can have unintended consequences (Åstebro et al., 2019; Cunningham et al., 2021). For example, Martínez and Sterzi (2020) found in the countries abolishing the Professor's Privilege that there tended to be a decline in the technological importance and the value of the patents owned and managed by universities.

Emerging literature points to some of the challenges governments also face when attempting to emulate existing examples. For instance, a study by Sandström et al. (2018) of public policies designed to drive academic entrepreneurship found success 'is contingent upon a number of factors such as individual incentives and capabilities, the goals of and trade-offs between different actors as well as a set of different contextual factors'. The authors concluded that it is 'difficult to emulate environments such as Route 128 in the Boston area or Silicon Valley as these contexts are highly specific', and recommended 'other mechanisms of transferring knowledge from universities to the surrounding economy' beyond attempting to recreate the famous examples.

Security issues are also salient in the third mission. As the research and third missions sit in the same security context as the teaching mission, we can see a parallel set of public policy interventions to those explored in Section 3. The use of export controls on research represents a response by governments to security threats. These controls typically apply to 'dual-use technologies' – those that have both civilian and military applications (Williams-Jones et al., 2014; Rychnovská, 2020). In 2020, Norway announced that its universities would need a licence to export knowledge made in the country (Myklebust, 2021). Japan recently strengthened its rules to address research interference amid growing US–China tensions (Mallapaty, 2020). In 2021, the intergovernmental political forum of developed nations the Group of Seven (G7) agreed a common position on export controls: 'The G7 affirms the importance of coordinated action to counter illegal intangible technology transfer, and protecting academia and business sectors from hostile state exploitation' (G7UK, 2021). Here, the state has to balance supporting science and its application with restricting into whose hands some of this science can fall. Considering the globalisation of science and the economy, restricting access to knowledge is challenging. The trend towards a stronger export control regime presents policymakers with other trade-offs. Japanese researchers are concerned that legitimate collaborations will be hampered. Export controls can be particularly difficult for small countries such as Norway, where cross-border collaboration is necessary to generate sufficient scale to undertake some research.

5.6 Measuring Impact and Engagement

Research points to the need for improved measures of the third mission. For example, Guerrero and Urbano (2019) find that a common problem when reviewing policy interventions is that 'it is not possible to understand if the expected objectives have been achieved'. This highlights the need for 'objective metrics associated with each policy frameworks and instruments', which 'are a crucial element for evaluating their effectiveness and legitimizing the role of policymakers'. This view concurs with that of Kochenkova et al. (2016) who point out the 'need for research to develop more precise and comprehensive evaluation criteria and thus obtain a more precise, better measured assessment of the effectiveness of different public policy measures'.

Evaluating the third mission is challenging. Primarily, this is because the third mission comprises a disparate group of complicated activities that have changed over time and are connected to both academia and applications in the wider world. People working in universities do not tend to practice the third mission; rather, they work on one part of it. In the last two decades, progress has been made to assess the performance of the third mission (see Molas-Gallart et al., 2002; Montesinos et al., 2008; Secundo et al., 2017). Considering the rising significance of the third mission, it was only a matter of time before the logics of contemporary approaches to governance would catch up with it. This can be seen in the growing interest among policymakers in applying performance measures to this mission (see SQW, 2019 for an example of the United Kingdom).

One overlap between the research and third missions that has gathered increased attention over the past twenty years is the non-academic impacts of academic research. These are the tangible benefits of academic research on the 'real world' beyond the academy. The Netherlands was a pioneer in the area of measuring the social impact of research. Spaapen et al.'s (2007) work on *Evaluating Research in Context* (ERiC) advanced ways of assessing impact in fields as diverse as agriculture, health care, pharmacology, and nanoscience; and served as a manual for those seeking to assess research impact and engagement. Through a process of back-and-forth policy transfer, the United Kingdom and Australia have both introduced an impact assessment component within their PRFSs and their grant application processes, making it an integral part of their research-funding regime (Gunn and Mintrom, 2018). Other jurisdictions have looked to do the same.

The efforts of the United Kingdom to assess the third mission are some of the most developed. The REF assesses ex-post the non-academic impact of specific, well-regarded published research. This assessment involves development of a series of case studies that must show a direct chain of causation between one item of research and some corroborated change in the world beyond academia. External (i.e. non-academic) experts are involved in assessing this component of the REF (Gunn and Mintrom, 2016, 2017). Research impacts only accounts for the part of the third mission that is anchored in the research mission. The United Kingdom launched its *Knowledge Exchange Framework* (KEF) to confront head-on the challenge of assessing the third mission. This provides the United Kingdom with a framework for each mission – TEF, REF, KEF – in what the government sees as three 'mutually reinforcing' evaluation frameworks. The KEF has seven component parts: research partnerships; working with business; working with the public and third sector; skills, enterprise, and entrepreneurship; local growth and regeneration; Intellectual Property (IP) and commercialisation; and public and community engagement. A majority of data is derived from the United Kingdom's existing *Higher Education Business and Community Interactions* survey. The KEF is assessed by metrics and written submissions.

Much value could be gained from enhancing common understanding among academics regarding the relationship between their chosen disciplines and society, what kind of work has impact, and how impact could be usefully improved. This does not mean that all researchers should strive for immediate relevance in what they do. But knowing how to better judge likelihood of impact can be useful for researchers planning their careers, for universities seeking to enhance their standing among peers, and for agencies funding research.

5.7 Conclusion

Universities have proven to be highly valuable resources for the societies and economies in which they reside. But there is much that universities contribute beyond what they do through the teaching and research missions. Those contributions, variously described as outreach, technology transfer, engagement, and so on, have here been discussed as 'the third mission'. Today, many universities around the world have structures and processes in place to support and encourage a wide range of interactions with people and organisations beyond the campus. Those interactions do not fall neatly into the categories of teaching or research or even applied research. And while revenue enhancement is always a motive in the university context, many of these interactions at the edge of the university have taken on a civic rather than a commercial complexion. We can see how various factors aligned to elevate the importance of the third mission within the university, and how this greater prominence created a challenge for policymakers in how to finance and measure these activities. Our discussion has emphasised the significant degree to which the third mission activities of universities have been driven by public policy. Governments have long sought to have universities contribute to society and to local economies in direct ways that are distinctive from their teaching and research contributions. Recent endeavours to measure the non-academic impact of academic research provides further proof of how governments seek new ways to shape what universities do and how they serve the wider world.

6 State Responses and Reassertions of University Autonomy

6.1 Introduction

The foregoing sections explored how public policies have been shaping each of the three missions of the contemporary university. In this section, we move to look at the university as a whole. This is because some of the responses of universities to their changing operating contexts do not neatly align with any of the three stated missions. It also enables us to complete the Element with a more holistic look at the university as an institution.

Changes to the university were highlighted in the previous sections – 'super-universities' driven by changes in the research mission and 'mega-universities' driven by innovations in the teaching mission. However, these are not precise categories but buzzwords used by commentators seeking to make sense of the disruption to the established order that they see around them. In this section, we show how the university as an institution is changing and the global influence of one model prescribing what a university should be. A reoccurring theme of this section is how universities are simultaneously competing and collaborating in contested territories. This can be seen in how institutions are connecting and networking with each other in new ways, leading to universities taking on new organisational forms. This can be where two or more institutions are formally merged into one, or, a looser arrangement, where multiple universities are members of an alliance. Given the theme of this Element, we need to consider if mergers and alliances arise 'organically' from universities working together or if they are orchestrated by policymakers with a political agenda.

6.2 The World-Class University

The World-Class University (WCU) is a product of globalisation and the greater global comparison that typically takes place in rankings. Altbach and Salmi (2011) identify three characteristics of WCUs:

> (a) a high contribution of talent (faculty members and students); (b) abundant resources to offer a rich learning environment and to conduct research; and (c) favourable governance features that encourage leadership, strategic vision, innovation and flexibility that enable institutions to make decisions and manage resources (2011, p. 3).

Although universities considered to be 'world class' are typically those with such attributes, they also need to display their status by performing well in rankings. Cheng et al. (2014) note WCUs 'play an important role in developing a nation's competitiveness in the global knowledge economy' and that their development 'is high on the policy agenda of various stakeholders across the globe' (p. 1). Literature has extensively explored the road institutions and governments have travelled to achieve WCU status. There are numerous examples, including Singapore (Xavier and Alsagoff, 2013), Korea (Jang et al., 2016), Indonesia (Sukoco et al., 2021), and India (Banker and Bhal, 2020), and this list is not exhaustive. Of particular interest to this Element is the role the state plays in this journey. In the eyes of the state, domestic highly ranked universities are now cast in the role of 'National Champions'. A National Champion is an 'enterprise selected by the government of a nation-state to spearhead the national effort to compete internationally in a particular industry' (Kumar and Steenkamp, 2013). In the post-war era, large national firms – such as *Olivetti* and *Michelin* – were the National Champions in the age of *industrial* policy (Owen, 2012). In the age of the knowledge economy, governments seek to place certain universities as National Champions in the current era of *innovation* policy. Just as before, states can play a crucial role in nurturing these flagship institutions within their jurisdictional bounds.

The WCU can be understood as a standard 'cookie cutter' model of what a contemporary university should be. A consequence of universities emulating one institutional type can be a rise in institutional isomorphism, and this has received attention in academic literature as introduced in Section 2 (Zapp and Ramirez, 2019). This makes the seminal work of DiMaggio and Powell (1983) particularly relevant when analysing higher education today. The authors set out how coercive, mimetic, and normative factors drive convergence in institutional form. Applied to higher education, this accounts for how the university is changing and how – in the context of the internationalisation – there is convergence around one ideal institutional type. Applying DiMaggio and Powell, we can see the following forces driving diffusion of the WCU model:

- Coercive forces: Universities are directed by the state to achieve certain objectives and perform well in global rankings. This is achieved through universities responding to government mandates or adjusting to the politically constructed environment within which the institution operates.
- Mimetic forces: Universities seek to emulate successful, recognised and highly ranked institutions to gain greater legitimacy in what is a status-conscious and esteem-driven sector. Practices that have worked for competitors will be adopted and emulated as universities do not wish to be outpaced by their peers. As DiMaggio and Powell (1983) explain 'Organizations tend to model themselves after similar organizations in their field that they perceive to be more legitimate or successful.'
- Normative forces: Globalisation of the academic profession and its 'norms' acts as an isomorphic force, through a process of 'socialisation', which is driven by greater international mobility. The professionalisation of university management and leadership has also been globalised both with the mobility of university elites and, with that, the mobility of ideas about how a university should operate.

We can see how the actions of the state align with the goals of institutions and the context of globalisation as universities seek to emulate the 'global gold standard' of what a university should be. Convergence around the WCU model should not be accepted uncritically. In a study exploring the 'international-level identities and models, national level policies and strategies, and institutional-level responses and practices' of the WCU, Li and Eryong (2020) found it to be 'an obvious Western-dominated value-laden paradigm'. This is in part because the WCU model follows the 'Emerging Global Model', which, as we saw in Section 4, originated in the United States and is therefore based on an American idea of what an elite university should be.

One key issue for the WCU model is its applicability to nations at different stages of economic development or with different academic and cultural traditions. For example, a WCU might be an expensive ivory tower and not be the optimal policy choice for a middle-income country pursuing a developmental state model with more practical requirements. Such trade-offs are rarely considered. Yet, pursuit of excellence as exemplified in the WCU model might result in significant missed opportunities for a state and, indeed, for a university. Excellence as understood and validated on the global stage might not align with domestic interests.

If we accept internationally recognised WCUs are an important and desirable feature for any nation's higher education sector, we can see a role for the state in creating such institutions in countries where this is absent. To address that gap, over thirty governments worldwide have launched what are known as 'Excellence Initiatives' (Salmi, 2016). These are government schemes when a number of universities are selected to receive additional resources to enable them to become a new national elite and rank on the world stage. Returning to the analogy of universities being the new National Champions, the process of selecting the universities to be included in an Excellence Initiative has similarities to 'picking winners' in the days of industrial policy. Excellence Initiatives are less applicable to countries that already have a highly differentiated system of universities such as the United Kingdom and United States, where elite institutions already exist and where higher education has traditionally been hierarchical and funding has long been unevenly distributed. The schemes have been more widely adopted in countries where universities have been more uniform, equal, and part of the public sector. The higher education sector in such countries may be strong, but it may not be organised in a way that is conducive to performing well on the global stage. For example, talent and resources might be spread across the system, rather than concentrated in specific privileged institutions. For universities in these countries, the state seeking to produce a hierarchical system with competition for funding and externally referenced criteria has represented a radical shift in the fundamental purpose of their organisation and the approaches to governance used to steer the sector. This can be challenging for universities not selected for the scheme.

Excellence Initiatives are typically state-initiated schemes, funding comes largely from the state, not from business or philanthropy. However, lobbying and support for such schemes can come from advocacy coalitions associated with the universities that are hungry for resources or want to build their own prestige. Here, there can be an alignment between political elites and university elites that drives policy change.

Excellence Initiatives have been pursued by a wide range of governments, including Malaysia (Noor and Crossley, 2013), Germany (Civera et al., 2020), and Spain (Seeber, 2017). In France, excellence was pursued through a large-scale restructuring of the sector that merged several long-standing institutions into one branded university that would then be in a position to achieve greater international recognition (Cremonini et al., 2014). This is an example of how government policies can result in new institutional forms.

As many Excellence Initiatives have achieved maturity, research attention has shifted to question if they have achieved what they set out to do and the wider effects of these schemes. This research includes investigating the positive or negative 'spillover effects' of a select number of universities receiving more resources (those selected to be part of the Excellence Initiative) on the wider national higher education sector. Nurturing a small number of potential WCUs may be 'the rising tide that lifts all boats' or merely drive inequality between universities in terms of level of resources and status. These are important questions for policymakers as we must not assume all government interventions simply go to plan, especially when dealing with the peculiarities of higher education.

It is important to note how Excellence Initiatives impact differently on the three missions outlined in this Element. Excellence Initiatives mainly seek to strengthen the research mission, perhaps at the expense of the other two missions. This is because the criteria in global rankings mostly relate to research performance. This may amplify the long-standing status and resource disparity between teaching and research within the academy. Some recent research has addressed the side effects of Excellence Initiatives on the third mission. For example, in a study of the German Excellence Initiative, Lehmann and Stockinger (2019) looked at academic entrepreneurial activity – patenting activity and industry collaboration – and found

> that the Initiative created an advantage for the whole of Germany while being an Excellence University does not have an impact on academic entrepreneurship with regards to patenting activity. However, we find a Matthew Effect concerning rewards in industry collaboration [i.e., a cumulative effect where to those who already have, more will be given]. We conclude that the Initiative had positive side effects for the system and partly also for the winners of the competition (Lehmann and Stockinger, 2019, p. 70).

A noteworthy case that highlights how research performance can be transformed is the Russian Universities Excellence Initiative, known as the 5–100 Project, which was launched in 2013. Initially, fifteen universities were selected to improve the global visibility of Russian universities. In 2015, an additional six were chosen. Since its launch, there has been a notable improvement in the ranking of Russian universities in both international institutional and subject-level rankings. This follows what Guskov et al. (2018) call the 'phenomenal rise' in research productivity and publication output in Russia. It is also worth exploring the more substantive effects of the scheme. Research by Lovakov at al. (2021) shows how the 5–100 Project has had structural consequences for the research mission of Russian universities. First, it has contributed, along with other government interventions, to a change in the 'role and place of research' in Russian higher education through greater collaboration between research and teaching. Second, the process of boosting research and competition in several selected universities has produced positive spillover effects for neighbouring universities outside the initiative. Matveeva and Ferligoj (2020) find a key driver within the 5–100 Project is collaboration. The authors find universities inside the project increased both their cooperation with each other as well as with foreign universities and research institutions of the Russian Academy of Sciences, while collaboration patterns of non-participating universities did not change significantly. This has been a factor in eroding the long-standing division between the two missions of research and teaching, which traditionally took place in different institutions in Russia.

An analysis of Excellence Initiatives would be incomplete without including China. China's WCU endeavours date back to the 1990s and have evolved from 'Project 211' then 'Project 985' to the current scheme 'Double World-Class'. It is beyond the scope of this Element to review the large volume of literature that has emerged investigating these Chinese schemes. Of particular relevance to this Element is research by Song et al. (2021). These researchers apply the concept of 'policy decoupling' – referring to when a policy is formally introduced but is not actually effective or implemented – to explain the institutional response to the double world-class project. The study finds that there have been some effects on the teaching mission in the pursuit of excellence, where some universities have closed or merged programmes in weaker academic disciplines. This has narrowed what is taught and reduced subject choice for students. Although there are no statements in government policy suggesting this, universities have closed programmes to help them meet WCU guidelines. Teaching quality may also have been hindered by the increasing number of 'shadow academics' that are being recruited to achieve a higher level of performance in global research rankings – but who are rarely, if ever, on campus and certainly do not teach.

Another aspect of the research by Song et al. (2021) illustrates the possible limitations on policy transfer in higher education. The authors point out that as China has been striving to catch up with Western countries it has been acting as a learner, continuously borrow[ing] policies from developed economies. . . It is therefore inevitable that a transplant rejection will emerge when foreign experiences are introduced into local contexts. Western institutions and policies are only partially learned and, at the same time, borrowed experiences must face a different institutional environment and political system (Song et al., 2021, p. 270).

The authors use this argument to explain why the implementation of a Western WCU model in the different contexts of China has resulted in some 'decoupling phenomena'. This reminds us that policy transfer between jurisdictions might be attractive to policymakers, but may not be the optimal strategy. A final consideration we must not lose sight of concerns the universities that the state has not included in Excellence Initiatives. For example, Hartley and Jarvis (2021) considered the Chinese universities outside the C9 group and found exclusion appears to be accompanied by 'reputational stagnation', which has implications for 'regional economic development, geographic diffusion of innovation, and workforce competitiveness'.

6.3 University Alliances

A straightforward way the university as an institution is being reorganised is through the merger of two or more into one, as occurred with the French Excellence Initiative. However, more complex and interesting arrangements are also evident such as alliances, which present the possibility for the study of what Ansell (2008) describes as Network Institutionalism, the analysis of networked relations among institutions.

In the world of higher education, we can observe alliances operating at different territorial scales. Alliances of universities within one nation state are longstanding. For example, the *Association of American Universities* (AAU), founded in 1900, still exists today and currently comprises sixty-three large research universities. Similar groupings of elite universities exist elsewhere, such as the *Russell Group* in the United Kingdom and the *Group of Eight* in Australia. These groups are effectively advocacy coalitions that represent the interests of their member universities to the state (Filippakou and Tapper, 2015).

As elite universities have evolved in other parts of the world, other groups of advocacy coalitions have emerged. An interesting example, which provides insight into higher education policymaking in China, is the C9 group. This emerged when the original nine universities in the Project 985 – the scheme to create WCUs in China discussed earlier in this section – were concerned in 2003 that their funding may be cut following a change in top political leadership towards one that favoured a more equitable and anti-elitist distribution of resources. The nine universities held a symposium to persuade national leadership that Project 985 must continue to enable Chinese universities to catch up with the world's highest ranking universities. They were successful in getting the Excellence Initiative extended several times to the benefit of their members (Liang, 2017).

Liang (2017) shows how this group of universities came together to discover common interests and were able to form a semi-formal advocacy coalition by navigating the political context of the PRC. However, C9 has been heavily dependent on the patronage of the Ministry of Education and its sustainability as a full advocacy coalition has been hampered by a domestic environment that leaves little room to manoeuvre. This highlights the interplay of knowledge and power in the university and state relationship in China. It is distinct from the dynamics observed in the United States, United Kingdom, or Australia, where advocacy coalitions and collective lobbying are a legal and accepted part of the policy landscape. Although China's elite universities are being funded to be global players with a degree of autonomy granted to them, their domestic actions are constrained by a tight regulatory regime and limits on collective action. This is particularly so with respect to their ability to lobby to change their domestic circumstances. This is a reminder that the ability of universities to form advocacy coalitions, and how such coalitions can be used, is dependent on the broader political environment.

Moving to a different territorial scale, there are global university alliances that draw on universities from several countries or even continents. An early example of this is the *Universities Bureau of the British Empire* that was founded in 1913 and would later become the *Association of Commonwealth Universities* that is still in operation today (Pietsch, 2013). Another important milestone in the development of global alliances includes the *International Association of Universities* launched in 1950.

At this global level, in recent years, we can see these existing alliances being joined by a new breed of alliances that are more strategic in intent. These alliances are typically part of an institution's internationalisation strategy, and membership is intended to aid universities to nurture their world-class credentials. These alliances usually do not undertake work to influence national policymaking. Membership of such alliances can be highly selective as universities only wish to be seen to be collaborating with institutions of similar status. They can be bilateral such as the Monash–Warwick Alliance or multilateral such as the *Worldwide Universities Network* (WUN), *Universitas 21* (U21), and the *Association of Pacific Rim Universities* (APRU). A study by Gunn and Mintrom (2013) investigated how WUN, U21, and the APRU were able to deliver distinctive 'collaborative advantage' for their members through working together. These alliances provide the structure for collaborations such as student or academic exchange as well as shared research projects. The APRU adds a geographic dimension as it seeks to assist university leaders to contribute to the integration of the Pacific Rim community of nations. Gunn and Mintrom (2013) highlighted how membership of these alliances is not just practical; it is a 'status signalling exercise' in a 'reputation race'. Moreover, members of these alliances were observed to climb more rapidly in global rankings than institutions that were not members.

Over the last decade, we can discern an international trend: university alliances have become fashionable, not just with university leaders but among political elites as well. This is evident in the growing number of university alliances. This collaboration is at a time of increased competition, internationalisation, and regional rivalry. At this junction, we can observe two types of university alliances.

1. Alliances that emerge organically from within the higher education community. Here, universities come together to collaborate in a process driven by university leaders – without state impetus or involvement. These alliances are often designed to generate strategic benefits (such as enhancing reputation through association with others) and/or operational benefits (such as greater academic mobility) for their members, which are universities who are invited and choose to join.
2. Alliances initiated by political elites and created by the state; entities that are a direct product of policy intervention. These alliances are intended to steer specific universities and shape the higher-education sector to achieve wider public policy goals. These goals can include but are certainly not limited to achieving greater recognition for some universities on the world stage or the exercise of soft power.

Whereas the first type of alliances may have been designed for universities to 'talk back' to the state – through lobbying on behalf of their member institutions – the second type, to a certain extent, do the work of the state. Two examples of the second type of alliances that were recently founded and have both had a strong regional dimension are the *European Universities Initiative* (EUI) and *Asian Universities Alliance* (AUA).

The EUI is a new regional network of universities that emanates from French President Macron's vision of a 'European renaissance', where he has argued 'we have neglected the solidarity between us ... The strongest cement that binds the European Union together will always be culture and knowledge' (Macron, 2017). These ideas can be seen in the high profile placed on European languages and cultures in the design of the EUI. The scheme complements existing efforts to ensure the economic competitiveness of Europe in the global economy, with a renewed emphasis on strengthening the identity and social solidarity of Europe (Gunn, 2020).

The AUA was launched in 2017 at Tsinghua University (a university prominent in China's higher education story, a recipient of WCU funding, and a member of C9) and is a multilateral alliance comprised of fifteen universities from fourteen countries. Initiated by the Chinese state, the AUA can be seen as an extension of China's 'One Belt, One Road' activities. It is a distinctly Asian enterprise, facilitating mobility across universities solely within the region. Moreover, the use of 'Asian wisdom' and the 'special traits possessed by Asian universities' to address regional and global challenges are seen as paramount to the AUA's mission (Cabanda et al., 2019).

We can see both alliances to be region-building projects with a clear geopolitical purpose, at a time when the global order is changing. This places universities within the exercise of soft power. It is important to note how a similar strategy is being pursued simultaneously by two rival regions. The development of the EUI and AUA illustrates how multilateral university alliances are regarded as an attractive and effective tool for policymakers looking to intervene in higher education to achieve certain goals, even in the diverse settings of Europe and China. The AUA is not the only Chinese university alliance: there is also the *University Alliance of the Silk Road* and *The Belt and Road and the Dunhuang Consensus University Alliance* (the latter is funded by the PRC's Ministry of Education, the former is not) as well as a *Silk Road Law School* alliance and a Sino–Russia university alliance, underscoring the prominent role alliances now have.

The regional nature of these schemes may also be of consequence as it may provide some regional nuance and variation to the WCU model in the future. For example, one of the aims of the AUA is to develop alternatives to the 'Western model' of the university and set out a different path for development. This could lead to a new 'regional bubble' for the diffusion of innovations in higher education policy in Asia, based on Asian ideas. If this was effective, it could possibly address the difficulties of policy transfer – what Song et al. call the 'transplant rejection' – where policy prescriptions taken from the generic WCU model developed in 'the West' are applied to Confucian settings and produce less-than-anticipated performance results.

6.4 Conclusion

As globalisation has advanced, and knowledge generation has become central to wealth creation, governments around the world have sought to ensure that universities within their jurisdiction perform well. In this section, we have discussed both policy interventions of states intended to promote university performance and initiatives taken by universities themselves. The international desirability of the WCU model, and the large number of nations pursuing Excellence Initiatives, is noteworthy as it illustrates the global diffusion of both policy goals and the policy interventions to achieve those goals. This section has also explained the dynamics that have been driving the emergence of new and changing institutional forms within higher education. A key theme of this section has been the importance of collaboration. Although the global higher education marketplace is increasingly competitive, we have shown how collaboration is being pursued by both policy-makers to achieve political goals and by individual universities as they assert their autonomy.

7 Opportunities for Policy Research

7.1 Introduction

Throughout this Element, we have shown how insights from contemporary policy theory can guide an analysis of the role of universities in society and, more specifically, how universities are shaped by public policy settings. In this section, we take the dilemma of how to more effectively portray the relationship between universities and the state as our starting point for identifying opportunities for future policy research. We discuss four matters we see as candidates for more research. First, we discuss the role of universities and the state in the global knowledge economy. Second, we consider how government priorities drive universities. Third, we address the issues surrounding measuring university performance. Fourth, we discuss institutional transformations. New research concerning these matters would help to generate better evidence about the role of universities in contemporary society. In turn, that evidence could support more informed future policymaking.

7.2 Universities and Knowledge Economies

It is impossible to understand the modern university without situating it within the broader political economy. We can see the modern university as a creature of the modern capitalist state and the geopolitical context within which both are situated. We can see the state has an enduring role in both the economy and university. This Element shows the applicability to contemporary higher education and the longevity of the ideas put forward by Weiss (1998) in *The Myth of the Powerless State*. We can see an enduring role for the state, and this Element acts as a counterbalance to the popular ideas of the all-encompassing 'internationalisation' of higher education. There are many examples of universities being subject to state direction and being tied to the increasingly intertwined economic and security interests of the nation.

The pressures of globalisation and the desire for nations to capture the perceived benefits of a global economy have changed the priorities of the state, and this is reflected in domestic policy. The state we see in Weiss's book is what Cerny (1997, 2010) calls the 'competition state', where, in the process of 'internalising' the effects of globalisation, the state takes on the role of ensuring the competitiveness of the nation on the world stage. Here, the competition state pursues reforms to make the 'economic activities located within the national territory, or which otherwise contribute to national wealth, more competitive in international and transnational terms' (Cerny, 1997, p. 259). This is more than governments reluctantly adapting to change; domestic elites often take a proactive lead in the process through policy entrepreneurship and coalition building. Moreover, the process does not result in a decline in state power, rather, state actors and institutions are intervening in new ways to deal with what they see as global 'realities', and, in doing so, are driving new forms of complex globalisation.

Because the university generates and stands at the centre of economic activity that contributes to national wealth, it has been reformed by the state to make it more competitive in international terms. We can see the universities in this Element not as 'state universities' (in the traditional sense of being financed or controlled by the state) but as 'competition state universities' (universities that serve the agenda of the competition state). The agenda of the competition state towards the university has evolved, and become more focussed, over time. In the 1990s, the knowledge economy and competitiveness narratives saw higher education generally increase in importance. Following this, new ideas on innovation resulted in an augmented third mission. The last decade has seen the pursuit of the WCU model.

The state can play a large role in innovation. Public funding of research in universities is a part of this. Public investments in research can end up in the products of private corporations. For example, the touchscreen on Apple's iPhone originates from research at the University of Delaware, funded by the NSF and the CIA. Although this is a good news story for the University of Delaware (Stewart, 2017), how a private company that pays little tax has benefitted from a public investment leads economist Mariana Mazzucato (2013) to point out 'We have socialised the risk of innovation but privatised the rewards.' This is because the state, exercising its 'entrepreneurial risk-taking role' through the university, takes the risks of funding research (and not just the research that goes to market) while business reaps the rewards through making profits. This illustrates how universities can sit between the state and industry in the innovation process.

The role the state plays in innovation and where the university is situated in this is an important research area. Policymakers need to give much greater consideration to who the beneficiaries of government-funded research are, that is, are some of the benefits contained within the nation and therefore serving competitiveness or is the public research merely serving 'the learning curve of the world'? And if the benefits do not accrue to the nation, will that affect the willingness of governments to continue to fund research? A related theme of growing importance is how policymakers create an environment that balances the national security of the nation (i.e. restricting and regulating the movement of knowledge and people) with international nature of the university (i.e. promoting collaboration and world-class validation).

Scholars of public policy have rich theoretical traditions to draw upon for guiding empirical research on these issues. Such research could explore how the narratives that frame policy decisions have changed over time, the advocacy coalitions that have promoted the placing of the university inside the innovation process. The current role of the university in the economy points to the value of interdisciplinary studies, for example, drawing on the political economy of innovation.

7.3 Universities and Government Priorities

Government priorities significantly shape the higher education landscape. The speed with which universities sought to develop a vaccine for COVID-19 offers a highly salient example of universities responding to the needs of the state. In 2020, we witnessed academics around the globe working in multi-university teams and collaborating with government health agencies, private foundations, and firms to understand the virus and how to inhibit its potentially deadly impact. No government bureaucracy or global consulting firm would have been able to make this contribution. This is an example of the state having the power, but universities having the knowledge. This is an important point to keep in mind, given the anti-intellectualism that characterises much political discourse and that is endemic in government advisory systems.

Government priorities have driven not only the funding of specific streams within universities but also the founding of new institutions. This is long-standing and predates the rise of the knowledge economy narrative. Historically, various episodes can be noted when governments realised that they were vulnerable to being left 'high and dry' unless they acted to promote higher education. In Australia, political leaders in the newly established colonies believed for a time that they could forego establishing universities and send their brightest young people to England to be trained in the professions. By the 1840s, it was clear that local demand for professionals would need to be met with a dependable local supply (Davis, 2017). This led to the creation of the University of Sydney in 1850 and the University of Melbourne in 1853. In the United States, anxiety prompted by the Soviet Union's launch of the Sputnik satellite in 1957 led to a rapid expansion of federal science funding. The era saw the expansion of university systems, such as the University of California and the State University of New York. As an indicator of this, Stony Brook University, part of the State University of New York System, was dubbed a 'sputnik university' when it emerged in the 1960s from being a small teacher training college into a major centre for scientific study (Geiger, 1997).

In the current period, we can see government's actively engineering structural change to their higher education sectors through fear of being 'left behind'. State interventions to nurture domestic WCUs can be seen as a policy innovation that has diffused worldwide. Moreover, Excellence Initiatives and state-sponsored WCU contenders show how the state is a complicit intermediary in the internationalisation of higher education. This need for international validation warrants further analysis. For example, studies of policy transfer can plot out how and why this perceived need spread around the world. This could also shed light on the narratives and advocacy coalitions in each jurisdiction that surround this motivation to emulate and achieve global recognition.

The connection between universities and government priorities more widely offers a fruitful area for further policy research. Such research could explore how political and policy choices have driven the evolution of specific universities and university systems. Research could also consider how the evolution of specific disciplines has been shaped by government priorities (following studies such as Kelves, 1978; Ricci, 1984). Such research could consider the political agenda-setting and advocacy coalitions and policy entrepreneurs that supported change. The role of political parties and ideologies, as well as approaches to public sector management and governance, should not be neglected. Such scholarship exists, but it is rarer to see theory-driven empirical work where policy theory has guided the development of research questions and conduct of empirical research.

7.4 Performance Measurement and Behavioural Change

We live in an era where performance measurement has become ubiquitous in society (Power, 1997; Mau, 2020). The arbitration of quality that has long given strategic power to bond rating agencies in the world of finance (Sinclair, 2005) has been emulated in many areas of the economy. In the process, consumers have acquired vital information to drive their purchase decisions. Governments have sought to fill information gaps, both to guide their future public invest-ments and to assist citizens to make more informed choices among service providers. But the introduction of performance measurement systems is also expected to drive behavioural change on the part of those entities subject to measurement; they shape the 'rules of the game' within institutions.

We noted in Section 4 the rise of non-government university rankings. The political power of rankings should not be underestimated. Mäkinen (2021) observes how 'rankings fever' has resulted in 'regimes and societies that would otherwise argue for their distinctiveness and sovereign decision-making' willing to give this up when it comes to universities as they 'accept the requirement of homogeneity to succeed in global university rankings'. Rankings have leverage as they are perceived to be natural, rational, and legitimate – even though academics tell us they are ordinarily none of those things (Ringel et al., 2020; Brankovic, 2021). University leaders and policy-makers take rankings seriously because the results are seen to have conse-quences (Hazelkorn, 2015; Stack, 2016; Benner, 2020; Dowsett, 2020). For example, a higher ranking makes it easier for a university to attract students, recruit and retain top academic talent, attract public and private sector organisations for partnerships, and secure funding from business and philan-thropists. These dynamics help explain the growing fixation in higher edu-cation discussions on the notion of the WCU model (Altbach and Salmi, 2011). Articulate university leaders and their advocates have used the exist-ence of global rankings to argue for greater government funding of their institutions. In doing so, they have made claims about the broader benefits – such as access to cutting-edge knowledge – that accrue to nations that are home to highly ranked universities. Here, the presence of high-ranking universities in a territory is seen as a proxy indicator of how well a nation can perform in the knowledge economy. This can explain why governments see the value in nurturing one or a handful of their public universities to attain world-class status (Mittelman, 2017).

We can also see how governments remain committed to measuring how well public universities perform with respect to teaching, research, and achieving external engagement and impact. This has resulted in the United Kingdom now having three sibling evaluation frameworks, one for each mission. We have seen that factors aligned to make research the dominant mission; one of the reasons for this being it is the easiest to measure and rank. It is worth noting the considerable progress made over the last decade in developing and refining approaches to evaluating the teaching and third missions. This may be a small step in helping these missions 'catch up' with the research mission by improv-ing how they are recognised and rewarded, leading to more balance across the three missions. Policy learning from this methodological work would lead to not just policy transfer but the evaluations of academic work being less arbitrary and more accurate in future. Although academics will understandably resist further evaluation, where it occurs it should be done well.

Several things observed in this Element point to the same recommendation: policymakers need to very carefully deploy measures of university performance. This is particularly acute as performance measures are increasingly attached to funding and carry reputation consequences. In designing these schemes, governments need to resist the temptation to impose excessive accountability systems or to micromanage research and development practices. In general, it is desirable for governments to focus their monitoring efforts on programme outcomes, rather than to dictate the form and evolution of processes. Policymakers need to monitor the multiple effects of performance measures on the higher education sector as a whole and the need to develop better measures should be regarded as a continuous exercise.

The behavioural changes engendered by performance measurement of universities present a rich area for further exploration, to which public policy scholars are well suited. First, thinking about rankings and achieving WCU status, the importance placed on this narrative has rapidly diffused around the world and perhaps without sufficient scrutiny. Much could be learned from exploring how advocacy coalitions in a given territory have appropriated this argument to frame the case for greater government support of specific universities – that is, how has the narrative diffused around the world? It must also be remembered that university rankings are not an actual measure of 'knowledge economy performance' (economies tends to be more complex than that) and the extent to which WCUs in a given territory do provide economic benefits should not be assumed but subject to research – that is, does the evidence match the narrative? Moreover, how do university leaders and policymakers respond to, or pursue, narratives that do not centre around developing WCUs? – that is, the alternative narratives to frame policy.

Second, considering government performance evaluations, it is worth questioning the drivers of these schemes and the public management ideas that underpin them. This also includes identifying any advocacy coalitions that may have influenced the performance criteria. Furthermore, there could be value in conducting comparative assessments of universities and other organisations to see how other sectors have driven changes in organisational behaviour (Blackman, 2021). This could look at how to minimise perverse incentives and goal displacement. Such research could ultimately advance our knowledge of when performance measurement systems are most effective at driving desired behaviour changes and when they are less effective.

7.5 Institutional Transformations

Alongside monarchy, ecclesiastical systems, and militaries, universities consti-
tute one of the longest-surviving institutional forms in modern society. But like
all those other long-lasting institutional forms, universities have gone through
massive transformations over the centuries. Although the roots of the large,
contemporary public research university can be traced back a long way, it is also
the case that these contemporary institutional forms would have been utterly
daunting to previous lions of university leadership like Woodrow Wilson at
Princeton University, Daniel Coit Gilman at Johns Hopkins, and Cardinal
Newman at University College Dublin. Universities have evolved, and in the
process, we have seen significant institutional transformations occur. Changing
government priorities, initiatives to measure and rank university performance,
and efforts to ensure universities effectively contribute to the advancement of
local knowledge economies, all hold the potential to drive changes in what
universities do and how they do it.

This Element has shown how the university as an institution is changing,
illustrating the relevance of historical institutionalism. In *'Elaborating the new
institutionalism': political agency (re)fashions institutional structures'* March
and Olsen (2011 p. 15) make an observation of such relevance to our discussion
that it deserves lengthy quotation:

> There are … situations where an institution has its *raison d'être*, mission,
> wisdom, integrity, organization, performance, moral foundation, justice, pres-
> tige, and resources questioned and it is asked whether the institution contributes
> to society what it is supposed to contribute. There are radical intrusions and
> attempts to achieve ideological hegemony and control over other institutional
> spheres, as well as stern defenses of institutional mandates and traditions
> against invasion of alien norms. An institution under serious attack is likely
> to reexamine its ethos, codes of behavior, primary allegiances, and pact with
> society (Merton 1942). There is rethinking, reorganization, refinancing, and
> possibly a new 'constitutional' settlement, rebalancing core institutions.
> Typically, taken-for-granted beliefs and arrangements are challenged by new
> or increased contact between previously separated polities or institutional
> spheres based on different principles (Berger and Luckmann, 1967, 107–108).

Here the seminal scholars of the new institutionalism, March and Olsen (2011) –
taking aspects from the more established work of Merton (1942) and Berger and
Luckmann (1967) – elaborate their theory in a non-applied way. Yet, within
these generic ideas, we can see a striking relevance to the contemporary
university as explored in this Element. We can see multiple instances where
the university as an institution has been questioned, not just by the state but by
other actors. Its performance has been questioned and then assessed, and this

has been used to determine its entitlement to resources. The prestige of universities has been questioned in terms of how they compete and rank on the world stage. Moreover, the ability of universities to manage free speech by themselves has been subject to challenge, and this poses questions regarding the moral foundation and integrity of these institutions that once seemed well beyond such contention.

The contribution universities make to society has been challenged, resulting in additional expectations being placed on higher education. Universities are now expected to serve the knowledge economy as a principal contribution. The state is one of the main drivers of this redefined contribution; where universities are a facet of industrial and innovation policy and serve a broader range of public policy priorities, rather than a narrower range of 'ivory tower' considerations. The state can exercise its power to ensure universities make the desired contribution. When considering the relationship between universities and the state, the funding and regulatory context can be seen as the 'primal environment' in which universities operate, and how this environment changes is an exogenous driver of institutional change. Here, the state indirectly steers universities through changing 'the rules of the game' and tinkering with the 'logics' of academic work. For example, performance measurement systems produce reputational and financial rewards that introduce new logics and disrupt established routines. Some institutions may be more resistant to exogenous change than others, which explains why international trends frequently have differing domestic consequences. We must remember there will also be other non-state exogenous and endogenous forces of change shaping institutional futures. What can actually be attributed to the state is an important research question.

The questioning of the university, and the reframing of how it serves society, has contributed to institutional transformation. This can be seen in new organisational forms such as multilateral alliances when institutions collaborate. Another dimension is the transformation of the activities within the university, emanating from the additional responsibilities, expectations, and shifting incentives. For example, the teaching mission is now subject to much greater accountability and transparency than ever before regarding what students receive and the labour market returns graduates can expect. Changes to the research mission were first observed in the 1990s by Gibbons et al. (1994) who argued the ways in which knowledge – scientific, social, and cultural – is produced and disseminated were undergoing fundamental change. This produced the idea of science needing to forge a new 'social contract with society' where 'science must leave the ivory tower and enter the agora' as knowledge must be not only 'reliable' but also 'socially robust' (Gibbons, 1999). In the ensuing years this trend has intensified, and it underpins the rationale behind the ever-expanding third mission, the research impact agenda being a particularly applicable example.

The changes outlined earlier can be seen as 'radical intrusions' that have to a significant degree redefined the purpose of the university and reordered the priorities within it. As the practices of the corporate world have been imported into the university, the mode of governance has shifted from collegial to managerial through which universities strategically seek to re-examine who they are and reorganise what they do. The nature of academic work, and what is valued, has changed, as illustrated by the shift to greater emphasis being placed on generating research income rather than pursing curiosity-driven scholarship. Previously taken-for-granted beliefs have been displaced fostering institutions that academics of previous generations would regard as alien.

The transformation of the university as an institution is an excellent subject for further, ongoing investigation. Historical Institutionalism can help explain how different types of universities have evolved over time, identifying points of resilience and change. How the fixation on the WCU model leads to institutional isomorphism could be explained by the coercive, mimetic, and normative forces as applied to the university in Section 6. It must be remembered most universities are not elite research institutions, and it might not be in the public interest for them to attempt to transition towards that model. Considering the commonality of this institutional type, the effects of Excellence Initiatives on universities *not* included need to be addressed by research. Research is needed into diversity in institutional forms, such as universities that are focussed around the other two missions.

Public policy researchers often consider the ways that policy changes lead to changes in the practices of institutions and the individuals within them (Rhodes et al., 2008). This powerful set of analytical tools helps us to not only explain how things are but also point to better policy interventions in the future. Those processes include deliberate learning from the successes and failures of others and changing conversations among political elites and advocacy coalitions (Mahoney and Thelen, 2009).

7.6 Conclusion

Throughout this Element, we have sought to clarify how public policy has shaped the development of universities and how it serves to shape contemporary institutional environments. This Element has demonstrated how policy interventions interact with trends in higher education that have profound influence on universities. Sometimes state intervention is welcome and justified. At other times it is neither. There will be times when universities need to acknowledge the obligations that accompany being based in a certain jurisdiction. While universities are often portrayed as autonomous organisations, they operate under rules, financial arrangements, incentives, and audit mechanisms established by governments. Even private universities must understand how governments shape their operating context.

This context needs to be subject to policy analysis. To make such research tractable, it is best focussed – in the first instance – on specific instances of change within a given jurisdiction. That kind of narrowing of focus allows for many potentially confounding explanations of the drivers of change to be treated as constants. As a result, opportunities emerge for research focussed on the interplay between the public policy settings established by specific governments and the choices made by university leaders as they seek to advance the interests of their institutions. Of course, careful, single-jurisdictional studies can lay the groundwork for development of cross-jurisdictional comparative studies. This can include studies of 'illiberal' or 'authoritarian' states that are exceptions within the prevailing liberal system as well as research into nations without the traditional Western models of governance or higher education. Burton R. Clark's (1983) claim that higher education systems are embedded in nation contexts that deserve careful comparison still stands in an age of internationalisation.

The higher education landscape is today being reshaped by new forms of disruption, creating new sites for the interplay of knowledge and power. New organisational forms and new patterns of competition and collaboration are evident. Here there are opportunities and threats. Universities will exercise their autonomy in the political and geographic spaces available to them. Disruption creates new imperatives for policymakers and potential new areas of intervention and regulation. Policymakers need to monitor new forms of higher education and plan for what this means for regulation in their territory. Policymakers also need to know how to nurture universities that meet national needs that involves appreciating the nuanced effects of internationalisation and calculating where it is beneficial and in 'the national interest' and where the risks outweigh the benefits.

For universities and the communities inside them, there is a pressing need to effectively articulate their case. They must use their knowledge as power to talk back to the state. This is particularly important when actors and advocacy coalitions who sit outside the academy are pushing narratives to influence what happens within it. This is illustrated by the recent politicalisation of free speech on campus.

In this section, we have highlighted opportunities for policy research. Much scope exists for new, theory-driven empirical research concerning aspects of the nexus of public policy and universities. Research needs to address who is exercising power over the university. If the state intervenes, whose agenda does it serve? Is the intervention justified, proportionate, and effective? What advocacy coalitions surround policymaking and what narratives do they use? What third parties are influencing the relationship between universities and the state? Such research holds the promise of strengthening our understanding of the role of universities in society. It also promises to improve the quality of the public policies being made to guide the practices of universities. It is critical that such research is undertaken. This is particularly pertinent as universities continue to globalise in an uncertain world with emerging security concerns.

The historical record shows the vital contributions that universities have made to the advancement of knowledge and the improvement of social and economic progress. As communities and countries around the world strive to improve the knowledge and skills of their citizens and to harness research-based knowledge, scientific discoveries, and technological innovation for better social and economic outcomes, this area of public policy will only grow in importance. To echo Vannevar Bush, we indeed face an 'endless frontier' (Bush, 1945). How well specific nations fare in the decades ahead will be determined to a considerable extent by how well they advance and harness knowledge. The interplay of knowledge and power must be carefully managed, and this can only occur when public policy encourages universities to be forward-looking organisations that attract and support cohorts of intellectually curious, energetic academics and students who understand their capacity to contribute to better worlds.

References

Abel, D. (2019). The diffusion of climate policies among German municipalities. *Journal of Public Policy*, 41(1), 1–26.

Acs, Z. & Sanders, M. (2021). Endogenous growth theory and regional extensions. In Fischer, M. M. & Nijkamp, P. (Eds.) *Handbook of Regional Science* (pp. 615–634). Springer

Adekoya, R., Kaufmann, E. & Simpson, T. (2020). *Academic freedom in the UK: Protecting viewpoint diversity*. Policy Exchange. https://policyexchange.org.uk/wp-content/uploads/Academic-freedom-in-the-UK.pdf

Altbach, P. (2003). The costs and benefits of world-class universities. *International Higher Education*, 33, 5–8.

Altbach, P. G. & Peterson, P. M. (2015). Higher education as a projection of America's soft power. In Watanabe, Y. & McConnell, D. L. (Eds.). *Soft power superpowers: Cultural and national assets of Japan and the United States* (pp. 69–85). Routledge.

Altbach, P. G. & Salmi, J. (2011). Introduction. In Altbach, P. G. & Salmi, J. (Eds.). *The road to academic excellence: The making of world-class research universities* (pp. 1–9). The World Bank.

Ansell, C. (2008). Network institutionalism. In Rhodes, R. A., Binder, S. A. & Rockman, B. A. (Eds.). *The Oxford handbook of political institutions* (pp. 75–89). Oxford University Press.

Åstebro, T., Braguinsky, S., Braunerhjelm, P. & Broström, A. (2019). Academic entrepreneurship: The Bayh–Dole Act versus the Professor's Privilege. *ILR Review*, 72(5), 1094–1122.

Australian Government (2020). *Tertiary Education Quality and Standards Agency Amendment (Prohibiting Academic Cheating Services) Act 2020*. www.legislation.gov.au/Details/C2020A00078

Bak, H. J. & Kim, D. H. (2019). The unintended consequences of performance-based incentives on inequality in scientists' research performance. *Science and Public Policy*, 46(2), 219–231.

Baker, D. P. (2007). Mass higher education and the super research university. *International Higher Education*, 49, 9–10.

Baker, D. P. (2008). Privatization, mass higher education, and the super research university. Symbiotic or zero-sum trends? *Die Hochschule: Journal für Wissenschaft und Bildung*, 17(2), 36–52.

Balbachevsky, E. (2015). The role of internal and external stakeholders in Brazilian higher education. In Schwartzman, S., Pinheiro, R. & Pillay, P.

(Eds.). *Higher education in the BRICS countries: Investigating the pact between higher education and society* (pp. 193–214). Springer.

Ballerini, V. (2017). Global higher education trends and national policies: Access, privatization, and internationalization in Argentina. *Policy Reviews in Higher Education*, 1(1), 42–68.

Banker, D. V. & Bhal, K. T. (2020). Creating world class universities: Roles and responsibilities for academic leaders in India. *Educational Management Administration & Leadership*, 48(3), 570–590.

Basu, A., Foland, P., Holdridge, G. & Shelton, R. D. (2018). China's rising leadership in science and technology: Quantitative and qualitative indicators. *Scientometrics*, 117(1), 249–269.

Baumgartner, F. R. & Jones, B. D. (2010). *Agendas and instability in American politics*. University of Chicago Press.

Bayma, B. A. (1979). Technology transfer: A public policy issue. *The Journal of Technology Transfer*, 3(2), 43–51.

Beech, S. E. (2019). *The geographies of international student mobility: Spaces, places and decision-making*. Springer.

Bekhradnia, B. (2021). The White Paper on free speech is intellectually flimsy. *HEPI Blog*, 17 March www.hepi.ac.uk/2021/03/17/bahram-bekhradnia-the-white-paper-on-free-speech-is-intellectually-flimsy/

Bekkers, R. & Bodas Freitas, I. (2008). *An evaluation of incentives and policies that affect research institutions' knowledge transfer activities*. Results of a paper commissioned by the European Commission, DG Research, as part of work by the Expert Group on Knowledge Transfer.

Bell, E., Fryar, A. H. & Hillman, N. (2018). When intuition misfires: A meta-analysis of research on performance-based funding in higher education. In Hazelkorn, E., Coates, H. & McCormick, A. C. (Eds.). *Research handbook on quality, performance and accountability in higher education.* (pp. 108–124) Edward Elgar.

Benito, M., Gil, P. & Romera, R. (2019). Funding, is it key for standing out in the university rankings? *Scientometrics*, 121(2), 771–792.

Benner, M. (2018). *The new global politics of science*. Edward Elgar.

Benner, M. (2020). Becoming world class: What it means and what it does. In Rider, S. et al. (Eds.), *World class universities: A contested concept* (pp. 25–40). Springer.

Berger, P. L. & Luckmann, T. (1967). *The social construction of reality*. Doubleday & Company.

Bhattacharya, N. (2012). The evolution of knowledge in the university. *The Information Society*, 28(4), 208–227.

Biagioli, M. & Lippman, A. (Eds.). (2020). *Gaming the metrics: Misconduct and manipulation in academic research*. MIT Press.

Bok, D. C. (1982). *Beyond the ivory tower: Social responsibilities of the modern university*. Harvard University Press.

Borgonovi, E., Anessi-Pessina, E. & Bianchi, C. (Eds.). (2018). *Outcome-based performance management in the public sector*. Springer.

Brankovic, J. (2021). Why rankings appear natural (but aren't). *Business & Society*,

Branscomb, L. M. & Keller, J. H. (1998). *Towards a research and innovation policy. Investing in innovation: Creating a research and innovation policy that works*. MIT Press.

Brennan, J. & Cochrane, A. (2019). Universities: In, of, and beyond their cities. *Oxford Review of Education*, 45(2), 188–203.

Bretag, T. (2016). Defining academic integrity. In Bretag, T. (Ed.). *Handbook of academic integrity* (pp. 3–6). Springer.

Brinkley, I. (2006). *Defining the knowledge economy*. The Work Foundation.

Britton, J., van der Erve, L. & Higgins, T. (2019). Income contingent student loan design: Lessons from around the world. *Economics of Education Review*, 71, 65–82.

Bush, V. (1945). *The endless frontier. A report to the president on a program for postwar scientific research*. Office of Scientific Research and Development.

Cabanda, E., Tan, E. S. & Chou, M. H. (2019). Higher education regionalism in Asia: What implications for Europe? *European Journal of Higher Education*, 9(1), 87–101.

Cantwell, B., Marginson, S. & Smolentseva, A. (Eds.). (2018). *High participation systems of higher education*. Oxford University Press.

Capano, G. (2011). Government continues to do its job. A comparative study of governance shifts in the higher education sector. *Public Administration*, 89 (4), 1622–1642.

Carroll, P. (2014). Policy transfer and accession: A comparison of three international governmental organisations. *Journal of Comparative Policy Analysis: Research and Practice*, 16(3), 280–296.

Ceccoli, S. & Crosston, M. (2019). Diffusion and policy transfer in armed UAV proliferation: The cases of Italy and Germany. *Policy Studies*, 40(2), 111–130.

Cerny, P. G. (1997). Paradoxes of the competition state: The dynamics of political globalization. *Government and Opposition*, 32(2), 251–274.

Cerny, P. G. (2010). The competition state today: From raison d'État to raison du Monde. *Policy Studies*, 31(1), 5–21.

Chapman, B. Higgins, T. & Stiglitz, J. E. (Eds.). (2014). *Income contingent loans: Theory, practice and prospects*. Palgrave Macmillan.

Cheng, Y., Wang, Q. & Liu, N. C. (2014). How world-class universities affect global higher education. In Cheng, Y., Wang, Q. & Liu, N. C. (Eds.). *How world-class universities affect global higher education* (pp. 1–10). SensePublishers.

Chong, D. & Druckman, J. N. (2007). Framing theory. *Annual Review of Political Science*, 10, 103–126.

Civera, A., Lehmann, E. E., Paleari, S. & Stockinger, S. A. (2020). Higher education policy: Why hope for quality when rewarding quantity? *Research Policy*, 49(8).

Clark, B. R. (1983). *The higher education system*. University of California Press.

Clark, B. R. (1998). The entrepreneurial university: Demand and response. *Tertiary Education and Management*, 4(1), 5–16.

Clarke, R. & Lancaster, T. (2006, June). Eliminating the successor to plagiarism? Identifying the usage of contract cheating sites. In *Proceedings of 2nd international plagiarism conference* (pp. 1–13). Northumbria Learning Press.

Clifford, M. & Kinser, K. (2016). How much autonomy do international branch campuses really have? *International Higher Education*, 87, 7–9.

CNRS (2021, 17 February). '*Islamo-leftism' is not a scientific reality*. Le Centre national de la recherche scientifique. www.cnrs.fr/en/islamo-leftism-not-sci entific-reality-0

Compagnucci, L. & Spigarelli, F. (2020). The Third Mission of the university: A systematic literature review on potentials and constraints. *Technological Forecasting and Social Change*, 161, 120284.

Conservative Party (2019). *Get Brexit Done, Unleash Britain's Potential*. www.conservatives.com/our-plan/get-brexit-done-and-unleash-britains-potential

Corbett, A. (2021, 23 February). Moral panics about free speech: How should European universities respond? *EUROPP*. https://blogs.lse.ac.uk/euro ppblog/2021/02/23/moral-panics-about-free-speech-how-should-european-universities-respond/

Corbett, A. & Gordon, C. (2018). Academic freedom in Europe: The Central European University affair and the wider lessons. *History of Education Quarterly*, 58(3), 467–474.

Craig, J. & Gunn, A. (2010). Higher skills and the knowledge economy: The challenge of offshoring. *Higher Education Management and Policy*, 22(3), 1–17.

Cremonini, L., Westerheijden, D. F., Benneworth, P. & Dauncey, H. (2014). In the shadow of celebrity? World-class university policies and public value in higher education. *Higher Education Policy*, 27(3),341–361

Croucher, G. & Woelert, P. (2016). Institutional isomorphism and the creation of the unified national system of higher education in Australia: An empirical analysis. *Higher Education*, 71(4), 439–453.

Crow, D. A. & Lawlor, A., (2016). Media in the policy process: Using framing and narratives to understand policy influences. *Review of Policy Research*, 33 (5), 472–491.

Cunningham, J. A., Lehmann, E. E., Menter, M. & Seitz, N. (2021). Regional Innovation, Entrepreneurship and the Reform of the Professor's Privilege in Germany. In Guerrero, M. & Urbano, D. (Eds.). *Technology transfer and entrepreneurial innovations* (pp. 175–205). Springer.

D'Arcy, N. (2020). Are essay mills threatening the integrity of academia? *University Times Ireland*. www.universitytimes.ie/2020/10/are-essay-mills-threatening-the-integrity-of-academia/

Da Wan, C., Lee, M. N. & Loke, H. Y. (Eds.). (2019). *The governance and management of universities in Asia: Global influences and local responses*. Routledge.

Davies, P. H. (2010). Intelligence and the machinery of government: Conceptualizing the intelligence community. *Public Policy and Administration*, 25(1), 29–46.

Davis, G. (2017). *The Australian idea of a university*. Melbourne University.

Davis, G., Weller, P., Eggins, S. & Craswell, E. (1999). What drives machinery of government change? Australia, Canada and the United Kingdom, 1950–1997. *Public Administration*, 77(1), 7–50.

De Boer, H., Jongbloed, B., Benneworth, P. et al. (2015). *Performance-based funding and performance agreements in fourteen higher education systems*. Center for Higher Education Policy Studies.

de Wit, H., &Altbach, P. G. (2021).Internationalization in higher education: global trends and recommendations for its future. *Policy Reviews in Higher Education*, 5(1), 28–46.

Diallo, R. (2020, 29 December). France's ideological wars have found a new battleground: Universities. *Washington Post*. https://www.washingtonpost.com/opinions/2020/12/29/france-academic-freedom-universities-backlash/

Diamond, L. & Morlino, L. (2004). The quality of democracy: An overview. *Journal of Democracy*, 15(4), 20–31.

DiMaggio, P. J. & Powell, W. W. (1983). The iron cage revisited: Institutional isomorphism and collective rationality in organizational fields. *American Sociological Review*, 48(2), 147–160.

Dobbins, M. & Knill, C. (2017). Higher education governance in France, Germany, and Italy: Change and variation in the impact of transnational soft governance. *Policy and Society*, 36(1), 67–88.

Dobbins, M., Knill, C. & Vögtle, E. (2011). An analytical framework for the crosscountry comparison of higher education governance. *Higher Education*, 62(5), 665–683.

Doidge, S. & Doyle, J. (2020). Australian universities in the age of Covid. *Educational Philosophy and Theory*.

d'Ombrain, N. (2007). Ministerial responsibility and the machinery of government. *Canadian Public Administration*, 50(2), 195–217.

Dougherty, K. J. & Natow, R. S. (2015). *The politics of performance funding for higher education: Origins, discontinuations, and transformations*. Johns Hopkins University Press.

Dowsett, L. (2020). Global university rankings and strategic planning: A case study of Australian institutional performance. *Journal of Higher Education Policy and Management*, 42(4), 478–494.

Draper, M. J. & Newton, P. M. (2017). A legal approach to tackling contract cheating?. *International Journal for Educational Integrity*, 13(1), 1–16.

Drinan, P. (2016). Getting political: What institutions and governments need to do. In Bretag, T. (Ed.). *Handbook of Academic Integrity* (pp. 1075–1087). Springer.

Duque, J. F. (2021). Who embodies the evaluative state? Programmatic actors in the Chilean and Colombian policies of quality assurance in higher education. *European Policy Analysis*, 7, 48–63.

Dynarski, S. M. (2021). An economist's perspective on student loans in the United States. In Neumark, D., Kim, Y. & Lee, S. (Eds.). *Human capital policy: Reducing inequality, boosting mobility and productivity* (pp. 84–102). Edward Elgar.

Enyedi, Z. (2018). Democratic backsliding and academic freedom in Hungary. *Perspectives on Politics*, 16(4), 1067–1074.

Etzkowitz, H. & Zhou, C. (2017). *The triple helix: University–industry–government innovation and entrepreneurship*. Routledge.

Equality and Human Rights Commission (2019). *Freedom of expression: A guide for higher education providers and students' unions in England and Wales*. www.equalityhumanrights.com/sites/default/files/freedom-of-expression-guide-for-higher-education-providers-and-students-unions-england-and-wales.pdf

Ferlie, E., Musselin, C. & Andresani, G. (2008). The steering of higher education systems: A public management perspective. *Higher Education*, 56(3), 325–348.

Filippakou, O. & Tapper, T. (2015). Mission groups and the new politics of British higher education. *Higher Education Quarterly*, 69(2), 121–137.

Fire, M. & Guestrin, C. (2019). Over-optimization of academic publishing metrics: Observing Goodhart's Law in action. *GigaScience*, 8(6), 1–20.

Flink, T. & Rüffin, N. (2019). The current state of the art of science diplomacy. In Simon, D., Kuhlmann, S., Stamm, J. & Canzler, W. (Eds.). *Handbook on science and public policy* (pp. 104–121). Edward Elgar.

Florida, R. (2002). *The rise of the creative class*. Basic Books.

Florida, R. (2005). *The flight of the creative class: The new global competition for talent*. HarperBusiness.

France 24 (2019, 28 March). *France faces blackface debate as students block Greek tragedy at Sorbonne*. www.france24.com/en/20190328-france-black face-racism-sorbonne-theatre

French, R. (2019). *Review of freedom of speech in Australian higher education providers*. Australian Government. https://www.dese.gov.au/higher-educa tion-publications/resources/report-independent-review-freedom-speech-aus tralian-higher-education-providers-march-2019

G7UK (2021). *Statement by the G7 Non-Proliferation Directors Group*. www .g7uk.org/statement-by-the-g7-non-proliferation-directors-group/

Gao, J. P., Su, C., Wang, H. Y., Zhai, L. H. & Pan, Y. T. (2019). Research fund evaluation based on academic publication output analysis: The case of Chinese research fund evaluation. *Scientometrics*, 119(2), 959–972.

Gaofeng, Yi., Krishna. V, V., Zhang, X. & Jiang, Y. (2021) *Chinese Universities in the National Innovation System*. Routledge.

Gardner, L. (2019, 17 February). The rise of the mega-University. *The Chronicle of Higher Education*. https://www.chronicle.com/article/mega-universities-are-on-the-rise-they-could-reshape-higher-ed-as-we-know-it/

Geiger, R. L. (1997). What happened after Sputnik? Shaping university research in the United States. *Minerva*, 35 (4), 349–367.

Gelber, K. (2020, 15 July). Is there a "free speech crisis" in Australian universities? *ABC Religion and Ethics*. https://www.abc.net.au/religion/katharine-gelber-free-speech-crisis-in-australian-universities/12459718

Geuna, A. & Martin, B. R. (2003). University research evaluation and funding: An international comparison. *Minerva*, 41(4), 277–304.

Geuna, A. & Muscio, A. (2009). The governance of university knowledge transfer: A critical review of the literature. *Minerva*, 47(1), 93–114.

Gibbons, M., Limoges, C., Nowotny, H., Schwartzman, S., Scott, P. & Trow, M. (1994). *The new production of knowledge: The dynamics of science and research in contemporary societies*. Sage.

Gibbons, M. (1999). Science's new social contract with society. *Nature*, 402, C81–C84.

Goddard, J., Hazelkorn, E. & Vallance, P. (Eds.). (2016). *The civic university: The policy and leadership challenges.* Edward Elgar.

Godin, B. (2004). The new economy: What the concept owes to the OECD. *Research Policy*, 33(5), 679–690.

Godin, B. (2006). The knowledge-based economy: Conceptual framework or buzzword?. *The Journal of Technology Transfer*, 31(1), 17–30.

Goldmann, K. (2005).Appropriateness and consequences: The logic of neo-institutionalism. *Governance*, 18(1), 35–52.

Gores, T. & Link, A. N. (2021). *The Globalization of the Bayh–Dole Act.* Now.

Graham, E. R., Shipan, C. R. & Volden, C. (2013). The diffusion of policy diffusion research in political science. *British Journal of Political Science*, 43 (3), 673–701.

Grimes, R. W. & McNulty, C. (2016). The Newton Fund: Science and innovation for development and diplomacy. *Science & Diplomacy*, 5(4). https://www.sciencediplomacy.org/article/2016/newton-fund-science-and-innovation-for-development-and-diplomacy

Grisorio, M. J. & Prota, F. (2020). Italy's national research assessment: Some unpleasant effects. *Studies in Higher Education*, 45(4), 736–754.

Grubbs, E. N. (2019). Academic espionage: Striking the balance between open and collaborative universities and protecting national security. *North Carolina Journal of Law & Technology*, 20(5), 235.

Guerrero, M. & Urbano, D. (2019). Effectiveness of technology transfer policies and legislation in fostering entrepreneurial innovations across continents: An overview. *The Journal of Technology Transfer*, 44(5), 1347–1366.

Gunn, A. (2015). The role of political and policy studies in higher education policy research. In Tight, M. & Huisman, J. (Eds.). *Theory and method in higher education research* (pp. 27–47). Emerald.

Gunn, A. (2018a). Metrics and methodologies for measuring teaching quality in higher education: Developing the Teaching Excellence Framework (TEF). *Educational Review*, 70(2), 129–148.

Gunn, A. (2018b). The UK teaching excellence framework (TEF): The development of a new transparency tool. In Curaj, A., Deca, L. & Pricopie, R. (Eds.). *European higher education area: The impact of past and future policies* (pp. 505–526). Springer.

Gunn, A. (2020). The European universities initiative: A study of alliance formation in higher education. In Curaj, A., Deca, L. & Pricopie, R. (Eds.). *European higher education area: Challenges for a new decade* (pp. 13–30). Springer.

Gunn, A. (2022). *Teaching excellence? Universities in an age of student consumerism*. Sage.

Gunn, A. & Mintrom, M. (2013). Global university alliances and the creation of collaborative advantage. *Journal of Higher Education Policy and Management*, 35(2), 179–192.

Gunn, A. & Mintrom, M. (2016). Higher education policy change in Europe: Academic research funding and the impact agenda. *European Education*, 48 (4), 241–257.

Gunn, A. & Mintrom, M. (2017). Evaluating the non-academic impact of academic research: Design considerations. *Journal of Higher Education Policy and Management*, 39(1), 20–30.

Gunn, A. & Mintrom, M. (2018). Measuring research impact in Australia. *Australian Universities' Review*, 60(1), 9–15.

Guskov, A. E., Kosyakov, D. V. & Selivanova, I. V. (2018). Boosting research productivity in top Russian universities: The circumstances of breakthrough. *Scientometrics*, 117(2), 1053–1080.

Harnisch, T. L. (2016). *Exploring the role of business-led advocacy coalitions as a strategy to elevate public higher education as a state funding priority* (doctoral dissertation). The George Washington University.

Hartley, K. & Jarvis, D. S. (2021). Let nine universities blossom: Opportunities and constraints on the development of higher education in China. *Higher Education Research & Development*.

Hawthorne, L. (2018). Attracting and retaining international students as skilled migrants. In Czaika, M. (Ed.). *High-skilled migration: Drivers and policies*. Oxford University Press.

Hazelkorn, E. (2015). *Rankings and the reshaping of higher education: The battle for world-class excellence*. Springer.

Hazelkorn, E. (2018). Reshaping the world order of higher education: The role and impact of rankings on national and global systems. *Policy Reviews in Higher Education*, 2(1), 4–31.

Hicks, D. (2009). Evolving regimes of multi-university research evaluation. *Higher Education*, 57(4), 393–404.

Hicks, D. (2012). Performance-based university research funding systems. *Research Policy*, 41(2), 251–261.

Hicks, D., Wouters, P., Waltman, L. et al. (2015). Bibliometrics: The Leiden Manifesto for research metrics, *Nature*, 520, 429–31.

Hillman, N. & Orosz, K. (2017). Introduction: Connecting student loan research and federal policy. *The Annals of the American Academy of Political and Social Science*, 671(1), 8–18.

HM Treasury (2003). *Lambert review of business-university collaboration*. HM Treasury.

Holgersson, M. & Aaboen, L. (2019). A literature review of intellectual property management in technology transfer offices: From appropriation to utilization. *Technology in Society*, 59, 101–132.

Huffman, A. E. (2020). Forgive and forget: An analysis of student loan forgiveness plans. *NC Banking Inst.*, 24, 449.

James, E. J. (1910). *University of Illinois; The University Studies, Vol. IV, No.1, November, 1910. The origin of the Land grant act of 1862: (the so-called Morrill act) and some account of its author, Jonathan B. Turner*. Urbana-Champaign: University Press.

Jang, D. H., Ryu, K., Yi, P. & Craig, D. A. (2016). The hurdles to being world class: Narrative analysis of the world-class university project in Korea. *Higher Education Policy*, 29(2), 234–253.

Jenkins-Smith, H. C., Nohrstedt, D., Weible, C. M. & Ingold, K. (2018). The advocacy coalition framework: An overview of the research program. In Weible, C. M. & Sabatier, P. A. (Eds.). *Theories of the policy process* (pp. 135–171). Routledge.

Jessop, B. (2018). On academic capitalism. *Critical Policy Studies*, 12(1), 104–109.

Jones, M. D. (2018).Advancing the narrative policy framework? The Musings of a potentially unreliable narrator. *Policy Studies Journal*, 46(4), 724–746.

Jones, M. D. & McBeth, M. K. (2010). A narrative policy framework: Clear enough to be wrong? *Policy Studies Journal*, 38 (2), 329–353.

Joo, Y. H. & Halx, M. D. (2012). The power of institutional isomorphism: An analysis of the institutionalization of performance-based pay systems in Korean National Universities. *Asia Pacific Education Review*, 13(2), 281–297.

Joske, A. (2018). *Picking flowers, making honey*. Australian Strategic Policy Institute.

Kahneman, D. (2012). *Thinking, fast and slow*. Penguin.

Kavanagh, D. & Richards, D. (2001). Departmentalism and joined-up government. *Parliamentary Affairs*, 54(1), 1–18.

Kay, A. (2005). A critique of the use of path dependency in policy studies. *Public Administration*, 83(3), 553–571.

Kelchen, R. & Stedrak, L. J. (2016). Does performance-based funding affect colleges' financial priorities? *Journal of Education Finance*, 41, 302–321.

Kelves, D. J. (1978). *The physicists. The history of a scientific community in modern America*. Knopf.

Kennedy, J. (2015, 13 April). Major universities crack down on cheats using MyMaster essay writing service. *ABC News*. www.abc.net.au/news/2015-04-14/major-universities-investigate-cheating-scandal/6390164

Kenney, M. & Patton, D. (2009). Reconsidering the Bayh–Dole Act and the current university invention ownership model. *Research Policy*, 38(9), 1407–1422.

Key, S. (1996). Economics or education: The establishment of American land-grant universities. *The Journal of Higher Education*, 67(2), 196–220.

Kim, S. K. & Yeom, M. (2017). An uncertain future: Leading national universities in South Korea and the flagship model. In Douglass, J. A. & Hawkins, J. N. (Eds.). *Envisioning the Asian new flagship university: Its past and vital future* (pp. 91–104). Berkeley Public Policy Press.

Knudsen, M. P., Frederiksen, M. H. & Goduscheit, R. C. (2021). New forms of engagement in third mission activities: A multi-level university-centric approach. *Innovation*, 23(2), 209–240.

Kochenkova, A., Grimaldi, R. & Munari, F. (2016). Public policy measures in support of knowledge transfer activities: A review of academic literature. *The Journal of Technology Transfer*, 41(3), 407–429.

Komuves, A. (2021, 5 June). Hungarians protest against planned Chinese university campus. *Reuters*. https://www.reuters.com/world/china/hungarians-protest-against-planned-chinese-university-campus-2021-06-05

König, P. D. (2019). A magic bullet in policy communication? On the ambiguous use of framing in policy research. *Policy Studies*, 42(1), 60–79.

König, T. (2017). *The European research council*. John Wiley & Sons.

Krishna, V. V. (Ed.). (2017). *Universities in the national innovation systems: Experiences from the Asia-Pacific*. Taylor & Francis.

Krücken, G. (2003). Mission impossible? Institutional barriers to the diffusion of the 'third academic mission' at German universities. *International Journal of Technology Management*, 25(1–2), 18–33.

Kumar, N. & Steenkamp, J. B. E. (2013). *Brand breakout*. Palgrave.

Laredo, P. (2007). Revisiting the third mission of universities: Toward a renewed categorization of university activities? *Higher Education Policy*, 20(4), 441–456.

Lazzeroni, M. & Piccaluga, A. (2018). The contribution of universities to the reduction of inequalities and to the development of peripheries: Insight from international case studies. In *Fifth Global Conference in Economic Geography: Dynamics in an Unequal World* (pp. 215–215). Global Conference on Economic Geography.

Le Monde (2020). Une centaine d'universitaires alertent : « Sur l'islamisme, ce qui nous menace, c'est la persistance du déni » Publié le 31 octobre 2020

www.lemonde.fr/idees/article/2020/10/31/une-centaine-d-universitaires-aler
tent-sur-l-islamisme-ce-qui-nous-menace-c-est-la-persistance-du-
deni_6057989_3232.html

Lee, J., Liu, K. & Wu, Y. (2020). Does the Asian catch-up model of world-class universities work? Revisiting the zero-sum game of global university rankings and government policies. *Educational Research for Policy and Practice*, 19(3), 319–343.

LeGrand, T. & Vas, C. (2014). Framing the policy analysis of OECD and Australian VET interaction: Two heuristics of policy transfer. *Journal of Comparative Policy Analysis: Research and Practice*, 16(3), 230–248.

Lehmann, E. E. & Stockinger, S. A. (2019). Entrepreneurship in higher education: The impact of competition-based policy programmes exemplified by the German Excellence Initiative. *Higher Education Quarterly*, 73(1), 70–84.

Leydesdorff, L. & Etzkowitz, H. (1996). Emergence of a Triple Helix of university—industry—government relations. *Science and Public Policy*, 23 (5), 279–286.

Li, J. & Eryong, X. (2020). Criticality in world-class universities research: A critical discourse analysis of international education publications. *Educational Philosophy and Theory*, 53(12), 1257–1271.

Liang, J. (2017). The enduring challenges for collective lobbying: The case of China's elite universities. *The China Journal*, 78(1), 81–99.

Lim, M. A. (2018). The building of weak expertise: The work of global university rankers. *Higher Education*, 75, 415–430

Lovakov, A., Panova, A., Sterligov, I. & Yudkevich, M. (2021). Does government support of a few leading universities have a broader impact on the higher education system? Evaluation of the Russian University Excellence Initiative. *Research Evaluation*, 30(3), 240–255.

Luger, M. I. (1991). *Technology in the garden: Research parks and regional economic development*. University of North Carolina Press.

Lumino, R., Gambardella, D. & Grimaldi, E. (2017). The evaluation turn in the higher education system: Lessons from Italy. *Journal of Educational Administration and History*, 49(2), 87–107.

Luxon, E. M. (2019). What do advocates know about policymaking? Revealing process in the Advocacy Coalition Framework. *Journal of European Public Policy*, 26(1), 106–125.

Macron, E. (2017, 26 September). *Speech on new initiative for Europe*, Paris. www.elysee.fr/emmanuel-macron/2017/09/26/president-macron-gives-speech-on-new-initiative-for-europe.en

Macron, E. (2020, 2 October). *Fight against separatism – the Republic in action*. www.diplomatie.gouv.fr/en/coming-to-france/france-facts/secular

ism-and-religious-freedom-in-france-63815/article/fight-against-separat ism-the-republic-in-action-speech-by-emmanuel-macron

Mäkinen, S. (2021). Global university rankings and Russia's quest for national sovereignty. *Comparative Education*, 57(3), 417–434.

Makse, T. & Volden, C. (2011). The role of policy attributes in the diffusion of innovations. *The Journal of Politics*, 73(1), 108–124.

Mahoney, J. & Thelen, K. (Eds.). (2009). *Explaining institutional change: Ambiguity, agency, and power.* Cambridge University Press.

Mallapaty, S. (2020, 4 August). Japan considers tougher rules on research interference amid US-China tensions. *Nature News*. www.nature.com/art icles/d41586-020-02273-w

March, J. G., & Olsen, J. P. (1989). *Rediscovering institutions: The organizational basis of politics.* Free Press.

March, J. G. & Olsen, J. P. (2011). Elaborating the 'new institutionalism'. In Goodin, R. E. (Ed.). *The Oxford handbook of political science* (pp. 3–20). Oxford University Press.

Marginson, S. (2021). What drives global science? The four competing narratives. *Studies in Higher Education*, 1–19.

Marhl, M. & Pausits, A. (2011). Third mission indicators for new ranking methodologies. *Evaluation in Higher Education*, 5(1), 43–64.

Marsh, D. & Sharman, J. C. (2009). Policy diffusion and policy transfer. *Policy Studies*, 30(3), 269–288.

Martínez, C. & Sterzi, V. (2020). The impact of the abolishment of the professor's privilege on European university-owned patents. *Industry and Innovation*, 28(3), 247–282.

Martin-Sardesai, A., Guthrie, J., Tooley, S. & Chaplin, S. (2019). History of research performance measurement systems in the Australian higher education sector. *Accounting History*, 24(1), 40–61.

Maskus, K. (2004). *The WTO, intellectual property rights and the knowledge economy.* Edward Elgar.

Matveeva, N. & Ferligoj, A. (2020). Scientific collaboration in Russian universities before and after the excellence initiative Project 5–100. *Scientometrics*, 124(3), 2383–2407.

Mau, S. (2020). Numbers matter! The society of indicators, scores and ratings. *International Studies in Sociology of Education*, 29(1–2), 19–37.

Mause, K. (2010). Considering market-based instruments for consumer protection in higher education. *Journal of Consumer Policy*, 33(1), 29–53.

Mazzucato, M. (2013). *The entrepreneurial state: Debunking public vs. private sector Myths.* Anthem Press.

McCraw, T. K. (2009). *Prophets of regulation*. 2nd ed. Harvard University Press.

McDowell, G. R. (2003). Engaged universities: Lessons from the land-grant universities and extension. *The Annals of the American Academy of Political and Social Science*, 585(1), 31–50.

McMillen, W. (2010). *From campus to capitol: The role of government relations in higher education*. Johns Hopkins University Press.

Medway, D., Roper, S. & Gillooly, L. (2018). Contract cheating in UK higher education: A covert investigation of essay mills. *British Educational Research Journal*, 44(3), 393–418.

Menand, L., Reitter, P. & Wellmon, C. (Eds.). (2017). *The rise of the research university: A sourcebook*. University of Chicago Press.

Merton, R. K. (1942). Science and technology in a democratic order. *Journal of Legal and Political Sociology*, 1(1), 115–126.

Mervis, J. (2019). Bipartisan bill proposes forum on US academic espionage. *Science*, 364 (6444), 922.

Meyer, J., Ramirez, F., Frank, D. & Schofer, E. (2008) Higher education as an institution. In P., Gumport (Ed.) *Sociology of higher education: contributions and their contexts* (pp. 187–221). Johns Hopkins University Press.

Mintrom, M. (2009a). Universities in the knowledge economy: A comparative analysis of nested institutions. *Journal of Comparative Policy Analysis*, 11 (3), 327–353.

Mintrom, M. (2009b). Competitive federalism and the governance of controversial science. *Publius: The Journal of Federalism*, 39(4), 606–631.

Mintrom, M. (2020). *Policy entrepreneurs and dynamic change*. Cambridge University Press.

Mittelman, J. H. (2017). *Implausible dream: The world-class university and repurposing higher education*. Princeton University Press.

Mizrahi, S. (2021). Performance funding and management in higher education: The autonomy paradox and failures in accountability. *Public Performance & Management Review*, 44 (2), 294–320.

Moed, H. F. (2017). A critical comparative analysis of five world university rankings. *Scientometrics*, 110(2), 967–990.

Mohrman, K., Ma, W. & Baker, D. (2008). The research university in transition: The emerging global model. *Higher Education Policy*, 21(1), 5–27.

Molas-Gallart, J., Salter, A., Patel, P., Scott, A. & Duran, X. (2002). *Measuring third stream activities. Final report to the Russell Group of Universities*. SPRU University of Sussex.

Montesinos, P., Carot, J. M., Martinez, J. M. & Mora, F. (2008). Third mission ranking for world class universities: Beyond teaching and research. *Higher Education in Europe*, 33(2–3), 259–271.

Moosa, I. A. (2018). *Publish or perish: Perceived benefits versus unintended consequences*. Edward Elgar.

Morris, E. J. (2018). Academic integrity matters: Five considerations for addressing contract cheating. *International Journal for Educational Integrity*, 14(1), 1–12.

Moscovitz, H. & Zahavi, H. (2019). The Bologna process as a foreign policy endeavour: Motivations and reactions to the externalisation of European higher education. *European Journal of Higher Education*, 9(1), 7–22.

Mowery, D. C. & Sampat, B. (2004). *The Bayh–Dole Act of 1980 and university–industry technology transfer: A model for other OECD governments?* Social Science and Technology Seminar Series. The Center on Employment and Economic Growth; Stanford University.

Mowery, D. C., Nelson, R. R., Sampat, B. N. & Ziedonis, A. A., (2015). *Ivory tower and industrial innovation: University-industry technology transfer before and after the Bayh-Dole Act*. Stanford University Press.

Myklebust, J. P. (2021, 25 June) Universities will need a licence to export knowledge, *University World News*. www.universityworldnews.com/post .php?story=20210625093913884

Nasution, V. I. A., Prasojo, E., Jannah, L. M. & Yumitro, G. (2020). Governance of autonomous higher education institution toward world-class university: A case study at the universitas Indonesia. *Governance*, 7(10), 2020.

Nay, O. (2014). International organisations and the production of hegemonic knowledge: How the World Bank and the OECD helped invent the fragile state concept. *Third World Quarterly*, 35(2), 210–231.

Neave, G. (2012). *The evaluative state, institutional autonomy and re-engineering higher education in Western Europe*. Springer.

Newcomer, K. E. (2015). From outputs to outcomes. In Guy, M. E. & Rubin, M. M. (Eds.). *Public administration evolving* (pp. 125–158). Routledge.

Newton, P. M. & Draper, M. J. (2017). University students are buying assignments – what could, or should, be done about it? *Impact of Social Sciences Blog*. https://blogs.lse.ac.uk/impactofsocialsciences/2017/02/28/university-students-are-buying-assignments-what-could-or-should-be-done-about-it/

Nguyen, C. M. & Choung, J. Y. (2020) Scientific knowledge production in China: A comparative analysis. *Scientometrics*, 124, 1279–1303.

Nixon, J. (2020). Disorderly identities: University rankings and the re-ordering of the academic mind. In Rider, S. et al. (Eds.). *World Class Universities, A Contested Concept* (pp. 11–24). Springer.

Noor, M. A. M. & Crossley, M. (2013). Educational innovation and the knowledge society: Development and issues of the clusters of excellence initiative in Malaysia. *Asia Pacific Journal of Education*, 33(2), 156–169.

O'Boyle, L. (1983). Learning for its own sake: The German university as nineteenth-century model. *Comparative Studies in Society and History, 25* (1), 3–25.

Ochsner, M., Kulczycki, E., Gedutis, A. & Peruginelli, G. (2020). 2.3 National research evaluation systems. In R. Ball (Ed.). *Handbook bibliometrics* (pp. 99–106). De Gruyter Saur.

O'Donnell, G. (2004). The quality of democracy: Why the rule of law matters. *Journal of Democracy, 15*(4), 32–46.

OECD (2005). *The measurement of scientific and technological activities: Guidelines for collecting and interpreting innovation data: Oslo manual,* (3rd ed.). OECD.

Olsen, J. P. (2007). The institutional dynamics of the European university. In Maassen, P. & Olsen, J. P. (Eds.). *University dynamics and European integration* (pp. 25–54). Springer.

Onishi, N. & Meheut, C. (2021, 15 February). Heating Up Culture Wars, France to Scour Universities for Ideas That 'Corrupt Society' *New York Times.* www .nytimes.com/2021/02/18/world/europe/france-universities-culture-wars .html

Ortagus, J. C., Kelchen, R., Rosinger, K. & Voorhees, N. (2020). Performance-based funding in American higher education: A systematic synthesis of the intended and unintended consequences. *Educational Evaluation and Policy Analysis, 42*(4), 520–550.

Osaki, T. (2020, 15 October) Japan boosts checks on Chinese students amid fears of campus spying. *Japan Times.* www.japantimes.co.jp/news/2020/10/ 15/national/crime-legal/japan-chinese-students-campus-espionage/

Owen, G. (2012). *Industrial policy in Europe since the second world war: What has been learnt?* (No. 1/2012). ECIPE occasional paper. https://ecipe.org/ publications/industrial-policy-europe-second-world-war-what-has-been- learnt/

Pelinescu, E. (2015). The impact of human capital on economic growth. *Procedia Economics and Finance, 22*(1), 184–190.

Peters, S. J., Jordan, N. R., Adamek, M. & Alter, T. R. (Eds.). (2006). *Engaging campus and community: The practice of public scholarship in the state and land-grant university system.* Kettering Foundation Press.

Pierson, P. (2004). *Politics in time: History, institutions, and social analysis.* Princeton University Press.

Pietsch, T. (2013). Out of Empire: The universities' bureau and the congresses of the universities of the British Empire, 1913–1939. In Schreuder, D. M. (Ed.). *Universities for a new world: Making a global network in international higher education, 1913–2013* (pp. 11–26). Sage.

Pinar, M. (2020). It is not all about performance: Importance of the funding formula in the allocation of performance-based research funding in England. *Research Evaluation*, 29(1), 100–119.

Pinheiro, R., Langa, P. V. & Pausits, A. (2015). One and two equals three? The third mission of higher education institutions. *European Journal of Higher Education*, 5(3), 233–249.

Pollitt, C. & Bouckaert. G. (2004). *Public management reform: A comparative analysis*. Oxford University Press

Power, M. (1997). *The audit society: Rituals of verification*. Oxford University Press.

Rewerski, P. (2007). The need for a new US stem cell research policy: A comparative look at international stem cell research laws. *Journal of Law, Technology & Policy*, 2, 415–431.

Rhodes, F. H. T. (2001). *The creation of the future: The role of the American university*. Cornell University Press.

Rhodes, R. A., Binder, S. A. & Rockman, B. A. (Eds). (2008). *The Oxford handbook of political institutions*. Oxford University Press.

Ringel, L., Brankovic, J. & Werron, T. (2020). The organizational engine of rankings: Connecting 'new' and 'old' institutionalism. *Politics and Governance*, 8(2), 36–47.

Ricci, D. M. (1984). *The tragedy of political science: Politics, scholarship, and democracy*. Yale University Press.

Ricci, P. & Civitillo, R. (2017). Accountability and third mission in Italian universities. *International Journal of Managerial and Financial Accounting*, 9(3), 201–221.

Robertson, S. L. (2009). 'Producing' the global knowledge economy: The World Bank, the Knowledge Assessment Methodology and education. In Simons, M., Olssen, M. & Peters, M. (Eds.). *Re-reading education policies: Studying the policy agenda of the 21st century* (pp. 235–256). Brill Sense.

Rogers, E. M. (1962). *Diffusion of innovation*. 5th ed. Free Press.

Rose, R. (1993). *Lesson-drawing in public policy: A guide to learning across time and space*. Chatham House Publishers.

Rosli, A. & Rossi, F. (2016). Third-mission policy goals and incentives from performance-based funding: Are they aligned? *Research Evaluation*, 25(4), 427–441.

Rutherford, A. & Rabovsky, T. (2014). Evaluating impacts of performance funding policies on student outcomes in higher education. *The Annals of the American Academy of Political and Social Science*, 655(1), 185–208.

Rychnovská, D. (2020). Security meets science governance: The EU politics of dual-use research. In Calcara, A., Csernatoni, R. & Lavallée, C. (Eds.).

Emerging Security Technologies and EU Governance (pp. 164–176). Routledge.

Sabatier, P. A. (1988). An advocacy coalition framework of policy change and the role of policy-oriented learning therein. *Policy Sciences*, 21(2–3), 129–168.

Sabatier, P. A. (1998). The advocacy coalition framework: Revisions and relevance for Europe. *Journal of European Public Policy*, 5(1), 98–130.

Sabatier, P. A. & Jenkins-Smith, H. C. (1993). *Policy change and learning: An advocacy coalition approach*. Westview Pr.

Salmi, J. (2009). *The challenge of establishing world class universities*. The World Bank.

Salmi, J. (2016). Excellence strategies and the creation of world-class universities. In Liu, N. C., Cheng, Y. & Wang, Q. (Eds.). *Matching Visibility and Performance*, (pp. 13–48). Sense Publishers.

Salop, S. C. & White, L. J. (1991). Policy watch: Antitrust goes to college. *Journal of Economic Perspectives*, 5(3), 193–202.

Sandström, C., Wennberg, K., Wallin, M. W. et al. (2018). Public policy for academic entrepreneurship initiatives: A review and critical discussion. *Journal of Technology Transfer*, 43, 1232–1256.

Saxenian, A. (1996). *Regional advantage*. Harvard University Press.

Saxenian, A. (2007). *The new argonauts: Regional advantage in a global economy*. Harvard University Press.

Scatamburlo-D'Annibale, V. (2019). The 'Culture Wars' reloaded: Trump, anti-political correctness and the right's' free speech' hypocrisy. *Journal for Critical Education Policy Studies*, 17(1), 69–119.

Schraer, R. & Butcher, B. (2018, 23 October). Universities: Is free speech under threat? *BBC Reality Check*. www.bbc.co.uk/news/education-45447938

Scott, J. C. (2006). The mission of the university: Medieval to postmodern transformations. *The Journal of Higher Education*, 77(1), 1–39.

Secundo, G., Perez, S. E., Martinaitis, Ž. & Leitner, K. H. (2017). An Intellectual Capital framework to measure universities' third mission activities. *Technological Forecasting and Social Change*, 123, 229–239.

Seeber, M. (2017). The international campus of excellence initiative in Spain. In De Boer, H., File, J., Huisman, J., Seeber, M., Vukasovic, M. & Westerheijden, D. F. (Eds.). Policy analysis of structural reforms in higher education: Processes and outcomes. (pp. 183–201). Palgrave Macmillan.

Sellar, S. & Lingard, B. (2013). The OECD and global governance in education. *Journal of Education Policy*, 28(5), 710–725.

Seyfried, M., Ansmann, M. & Pohlenz, P. (2019). Institutional isomorphism, entrepreneurship and effectiveness: The adoption and implementation of quality management in teaching and learning in Germany. *Tertiary Education and Management,* 25(2), 115–129.

Shah, M., Bennett, A., & Southgate, E. (2015). *Widening higher education participation: A global perspective.* Chandos Publishing.

Shanahan, E. A., Jones, M. D. & McBeth, M. K. (2018). How to conduct a narrative policy framework study. *The Social Science Journal,* 55(3), 332–345.

Shanahan, E. A., Raile, E. D., French, K. A. & McEvoy, J. (2018). Bounded stories. *Policy Studies Journal,* 46(4), 922–948.

Shane, S. (2004). *Academic entrepreneurship: University spinoffs and wealth creation.* Edward Elgar.

Sim, W. (2020, 5 October). Japan to tighten checks on visa applications by Chinese students, researchers over espionage concerns: Report. *The Straits Times.* www.straitstimes.com/asia/east-asia/japan-to-tighten-checks-on-visa-applications-by-chinese-students-researchers-over

Simmons, B. A., Dobbin, F. & Garrett, G. (2006). Introduction: The international diffusion of liberalism. *International Organization,* 60(4), 781–810.

Sinclair, T. J. (2005). *The new masters of capital: American bond rating agencies and the politics of creditworthiness.* Cornell University Press.

Slaughter, S. & Leslie, L. L. (1997). *Academic capitalism: Politics, policies, and the entrepreneurial university.* John Hopkins University Press

Slaughter, S. A. & Rhoades, G. (2004). *Academic capitalism and the new economy: Markets, state, and higher education.* John Hopkins University Press.

Song, J., Chu, Z. & Xu, Y. (2021). Policy decoupling in strategic response to the double world-class project: evidence from elite universities in China. *Higher Education,* 82(2), 255–272.

Spaapen, J., Dijstelbloem, H. & Wamelink, F. (2007). *Evaluating research in context. A method for comprehensive assessment,* 2nd ed. COS The Hague.

Spooner, M. (2019, October). Performance–based funding in higher education. *CAUT Education Review.* www.caut.ca/sites/default/files/caut–education–review–performance–based_funding_in_higher_education.pdf

Spooner, M. (2021). COVID-19 Reveals the folly of performance-based funding for universities. *The Conversation.* https://theconversation.com/covid-19-reveals-the-folly-of-performance-based-funding-for-universities-138575

Stack, M. (2016). *Global university rankings and the Mediatization of higher education.* Palgrave Macmillan.

Staley, J. (2019). University of Chicago: A free speech experiment. *Legacy,* 19 (1), 47–61.

Staton, B. Warrell, H. & Cameron-Chileshe, J. (2021, 20 February). UK academics struggle with stricter security on China, *The FT*. www.ft.com/content/ce587d32-1c1e-4f03-93bd-846379ed993d

Stewart, J. (2017, 15 September). A culture of innovation. *UDaily*. www.udel.edu/udaily/2017/september/engineering-iphone-fingerworks/

Stockman, F. &Mureithi, C. (2019, 9 July). Cheating, Inc.: How writing papers for American college students has become a lucrative profession overseas. *New York Times*. https://www.nytimes.com/2019/09/07/us/college-cheating-papers.html

Stokes, D. E. (1997). *Pasteur's quadrant: Basic science and technological innovation*. Brookings Institution.

Stone, D. (2012). *Policy paradox: The art of political decision making* (3rd ed.). W. W. Norton & Company.

Stone, D. (2019). *Making global policy*. Cambridge University Press.

Strandburg, K. J. (2005). Curiosity-driven research and university technology transfer. In Libecap, G. D. (Ed.) *University entrepreneurship and technology transfer: Process, design, and intellectual property. Advances in the Study of Entrepreneurship, Innovation and Economic Growth*, Vol 16 (pp. 93–122). Elsevier.

SQW (2019). Knowledge exchange funding: A review of novel evaluation methodologies. *Research England*. https://re.ukri.org/sector-guidance/publications/knowledge-exchange-funding-a-review-of-novel-evaluation-methodologies-report/

Sukoco, B. M., Mudzakkir, M. F., Ubaidi, A. et al. (2021). Stakeholder pressure to obtain world-class status among Indonesian universities. *Higher Education*, 82, 561–581.

Takeo, Y. & Urabe, E. (2021, 19 January). Japan to start $96 billion university fund by March 2022. *Bloomberg*. www.bloomberg.com/news/articles/2021-01-19/japan-to-start-96-billion-university-fund-by-march-2022

Teixeira, P., Rocha, V., Biscaia, R. &Cardoso, M. F. (2014).Policy changes, marketisation trends and spatial dispersion in European higher education: Comparing public and private sectors. *Cambridge Journal of Regions, Economy and Society*, 7(2), 271–288.

Thelen, K. & Conran, J. (2016). Institutional change. In Fioretos, O., Falleti, T. G. & Sheingate, A. (Eds.). *The Oxford handbook of historical institutionalism* (pp. 51–70). Oxford University Press.

Thomas, D. A., Nedeva, M., Tirado, M. M. & Jacob, M. (2020). Changing research on research evaluation: A critical literature review to revisit the agenda. *Research Evaluation*, 29(3), 275–288.

Thomas, E. & Pugh, R. (2020). From 'entrepreneurial' to 'engaged' universities: Social innovation for regional development in the Global South. *Regional Studies*, 54(12), 1631–1643.

Thursby, J. G. & Thursby, M. C. (2002). Who is selling the ivory tower? Sources of growth in university licensing. *Management Science*, 48, 90–104.

Tierney, W. (2012). Regulating private for-profit higher education. *International Higher Education*, 69, 5–7.

Togoh, I. (2020, 10 September). China reacts as U.S. revokes visas of more than 1,000 'high-risk' Chinese students. *Forbes*. www.forbes.com/sites/isabelto goh/2020/09/10/china-reacts-as-us-revokes-visas-of-more-than-1000-high-risk-chinese-students/

Tollefson, J. (2018). China declared world's largest producer of scientific articles. *Nature*, 553(7686), 390–391.

True, J. & Mintrom, M., (2001). Transnational networks and policy diffusion: The case of gender mainstreaming. *International Studies Quarterly*, 45(1), 27–57.

Universities Australia (2018, 26 October). *There's no place for political interference in Australian research funding*. www.universitiesaustralia.edu.au/media-item/theres-no-place-for-political-interference-in-australian-research-funding/

Uscinski, J. E. & Klofstad, C. A. (2013). Determinants of representatives' votes on the flake amendment to end national science foundation funding of political science research. *PS: Political Science & Politics*, 46(3), 557–561.

Van der Steen, M. & Enders, J. (2008). Universities in evolutionary systems of innovation. *Creativity and Innovation Management*, 17 (4), 281–292.

Van Hulst, M. & Yanow, D. (2016). From policy 'frames' to 'framing' theorizing a more dynamic, political approach. The *American Review of Public Administration*, 46(1), 92–112.

Vorley, T. & Nelles, J. (2008). (Re) conceptualising the academy: Institutional development of and beyond the third mission. *Higher Education Management and Policy*, 20(3), 1–17.

Walker, J. L. (1969). The diffusion of innovations among the American states. *American Political Science Review*, 63(3), 880–899.

Walker, M. & Townley, C. (2012). Contract cheating: A new challenge for academic honesty? *Journal of Academic Ethics*, 10(1), 27–44.

Wang, L., Wang, X., Piro, F. N. & Philipsen, N. (2020). The effect of competitive public funding on scientific output. *Research Evaluation*, 29 (4), 418–429.

Warikoo, N. & Allen, U. (2020). A solution to multiple problems: The origins of affirmative action in higher education around the world. *Studies in Higher Education*, 45(12), 2398–2412.

Washburn, J. (2005). *University Inc.: The corporate corruption of higher education*. Basic Books.

Weible, C. M., Ingold, K., Nohrstedt, D., Henry, A. D. & Jenkins-Smith, H. C. (2020). Sharpening advocacy coalitions. *Policy Studies Journal*, 48(4), 1054–1081.

Weible, C. M. & Sabatier, P. A. (2018). *Theories of the policy process*. Routledge.

Weiss, L. (1998). *The myth of the powerless state*. Cornell University Press.

Williams-Jones, B., Olivier, C. & Smith, E. (2014). Governing 'dual-use' research in Canada: A policy review. *Science and Public Policy, 41*(1), 76–93.

Wilsdon, J., Allen, L., Belfiore, E. et al. (2015). *The metric tide: report of the independent review of the role of metrics in research assessment and management*. Sage.

Wojciuk, A. (2018). *Empires of knowledge in international relations: Education and science as sources of power for the state*. Routledge.

Xavier, C. A. & Alsagoff, L. (2013). Constructing 'world-class' as 'global': A case study of the National University of Singapore. *Educational Research for Policy and Practice*, 12(3), 225–238.

Xu, X. (2020). Performing under 'the baton of administrative power'? Chinese academics' responses to incentives for international publications. *Research Evaluation*, 29(1), 87–99.

Yonezawa, A., Hammond, C. D., Brotherhood, T., Kitamura, M. & Kitagawa, F. (2020). Evolutions in knowledge production policy and practice in Japan: A case study of an interdisciplinary research institute for disaster science. *Journal of Higher Education Policy and Management*, 42(2), 230–244.

Zacharewicz, T., Lepori, B., Reale, E. & Jonkers, K. (2019). Performance-based research funding in EU Member States—a comparative assessment. *Science and Public Policy*, 46(1), 105–115.

Zapp, M. & Ramirez, F. O. (2019). Beyond internationalisation and isomorphism–the construction of a global higher education regime. *Comparative Education*, 55(4),473–493.

Zhou, P., Cai, X. & Lyu, X. (2020). An in-depth analysis of government funding and international collaboration in scientific research. *Scientometrics*, 125(2), 1331–1347.

Acknowledgements

This Element had its origins in a series of collaborations that began when Andrew S. Gunn visited the University of Auckland from the University of Leeds on a Worldwide Universities Network scholarship. Michael Mintrom gained rich insights into the nature of university alliances with off-campus entities through funds made available by the University of Auckland and Universitas 21. We both benefitted from generous research and travel support from the Australia and New Zealand School of Government (ANZSOG) when we initiated this project. We are especially grateful to Michael P. Howlett and M. Ramesh for their encouragement and advice as we shaped the design of this Element. Andrew Gunn is grateful to Worldwide Universities Network member the University of Leeds for funding the international mobility that fostered the collaboration that produced this publication. He is also grateful to the Worldwide Universities Network, particularly the activities of the Global Higher Education and Research challenge, for supporting and inspiring his research over several years. Andrew would also like to thank Better Governance and Policy colleagues at Monash University for their encouragement. Michael Mintrom is grateful to Michigan State University, the University of Auckland, and Monash University for the many opportunities they each provided him to investigate how universities engage with the world around them. He especially benefitted from serving as Associate Dean of Arts for Research performance at the University of Auckland and as Associate Dean of Arts for Enterprise at Monash University. Both Michael and Andrew thank our many colleagues for their advice and support as we wrote this Element. We give special mention to Professor Ken Smith AO, CEO and Dean of ANZSOG, and Professor Glyn Davis, former Vice-Chancellor of the University of Melbourne. Finally, we wish to thank our families for giving us the time and support to complete the writing of this Element, often in evenings and weekends.

Cambridge Elements ☰

Public Policy

M. Ramesh

National University of Singapore (NUS)

M. Ramesh is UNESCO Chair on Social Policy Design at the Lee Kuan Yew School of Public Policy, NUS. His research focuses on governance and social policy in East and Southeast Asia, in addition to public policy institutions and processes. He has published extensively in reputed international journals. He is Co-editor of *Policy and Society and Policy Design and Practice.*

Michael Howlett

Simon Fraser University, British Colombia

Michael Howlett is Burnaby Mountain Professor and Canada Research Chair (Tier 1) in the Department of Political Science, Simon Fraser University. He specialises in public policy analysis, and resource and environmental policy. He is currently editor-in-chief of *Policy Sciences* and co-editor of the *Journal of Comparative Policy Analysis, Policy and Society and Policy Design and Practice.*

Xun WU

Hong Kong University of Science and Technology

Xun WU is Professor and Head of the Division of Public Policy at the Hong Kong University of Science and Technology. He is a policy scientist whose research interests include policy innovations, water resource management and health policy reform. He has been involved extensively in consultancy and executive education, his work involving consultations for the World Bank and UNEP.

Judith Clifton

University of Cantabria

Judith Clifton is Professor of Economics at the University of Cantabria, Spain. She has published in leading policy journals and is editor-in-chief of the *Journal of Economic Policy Reform.* Most recently, her research enquires how emerging technologies can transform public administration, a forward-looking cutting-edge project which received €3.5 million funding from the Horizon2020 programme.

Eduardo Araral

National University of Singapore (NUS)

Eduardo Araral is widely published in various journals and books and has presented in forty conferences. He is currently Co-Director of the Institute of Water Policy at the Lee Kuan Yew School of Public Policy, NUS, and is a member of the editorial board of *Journal of Public Administration Research and Theory* and the board of the Public Management Research Association.

About the Series

Elements in Public Policy is a concise and authoritative collection of assessments of the state of the art and future research directions in public policy research, as well as substantive new research on key topics. Edited by leading scholars in the field, the series is an ideal medium for reflecting on and advancing the understanding of critical issues in the public sphere. Collectively, the series provides a forum for broad and diverse coverage of all major topics in the field while integrating different disciplinary and methodological approaches.

Cambridge Elements ≡

Public Policy

.

Printed in Great Britain
by Amazon

45107557R00059